PORSCHE
356

First published in 1996 by Veloce Publishing Ltd., 33 Trinity Street, Dorchester DT1 1TT, England. Fax: 01305 268864.
E-mail: info@veloce.co.uk. Reprinted as paperback edition 2002.

Cover front panel picture: Porsche 356 Speedster Carrera 1500 courtesy of *Classic and Sportscar* magazine.

PORSCHE
356

BRIAN LONG

VELOCE PUBLISHING
THE PUBLISHER OF FINE AUTOMOTIVE BOOKS

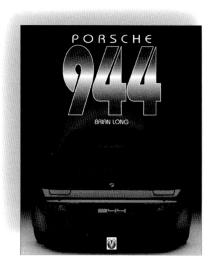
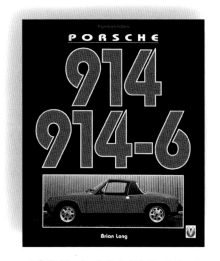
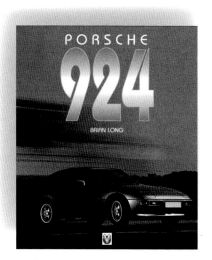
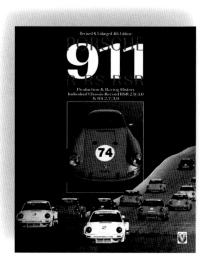

CONTENTS

PREFACE

The Porsche 356 is one of those models that evokes two completely different reactions. To some, it's little more than a bloated Volkswagen Beetle; to others, who know the car, it's a very special machine.

What is so special? In a nutshell it's the depth of design and engineering: the care that was taken with every single component - quality is the key (who else but Porsche would have run-in the steering gear before it was put on the car to ensure it was perfect for the customer?) The 356 also inspired a hugely-successful breed of racing cars and then benefited from the race-proven technology in its production road car applications.

Throughout the book photo-graphs (even the majority of pictures in the Colour Gallery) con-temporaneous with the original cars have been used to aid authenticity. Some of these older pictures have poor tonal balance or focus, but the author feels that their historical importance outweighs these shortcomings.

The author has always been a Porsche fan, and regards it as a privilege to have received so much help from Klaus Parr and his team in the archive department at the Porsche factory. The Porsche archive department supplied much useful information and the majority of the photographs used in this book.

Brian Long
Coventry, England

PORSCHE 356

1

BIRTH
OF A
LEGEND

As with so many famous marques, the story behind the foundation of Porsche is largely the story of one man - in this case Professor Ferdinand Porsche. However, the sports cars on which today's Porsche legend has been built are the work of his son, Dr. Ing. h.c. Ferry Porsche and, although this book concerns itself with Ferry Porsche's machines, it is only right that a few words should be said on the origins of the Stuttgart marque.

Ferdinand Porsche was born on 3 September 1875. The son of a tinsmith, he grew up in the village of Maffersdorf, receiving his early education there before moving on to the Reichenberg State Technical School to study electrical-technology.

Shortly after his eighteenth birthday, he left the family home for Vienna and, by 1897, he had already built himself an electric-powered bicycle whilst in the employ of Bela Egger & Co. In 1899, Porsche joined Jakob Lohner, whose interest in electric cars and vast experience in the carriage trade led to the Lohner-Porsche motor car. This novel design (first shown

The Lohner-Porsche, which had a surprising amount of competition success. This is the first one built, dating from 1900.

One of the "Sascha" Austro-Daimlers, as used on the 1922 Targa Florio.

at the 1900 Paris Exhibition), featuring an electric motor in each front wheel hub, would set Porsche on a path of automobile design. An interesting story relating to this car concerns Porsche's National Service in 1902 - during this time, he was actually the chauffeur for Archduke Franz Ferdinand, whose preferred transport was a Lohner-Porsche!

Porsche married in 1903 and, in 1905, he left Lohner to take up the appointment of Technical Director at Austro-Daimler, the Austrian arm of the Daimler Motoren Gesellschaft. Porsche designed a number of vehicles for the company (including the famous car which later became known as the "Prince Henry" model following its

great success in the 1910 Trials of that name) and also moved them towards aero-engine production.

During the First World War, Porsche's mixed-drive motors powered a number of supply trains and artillery tractors. When a captured Austro-Daimler engine was examined by the Allied authorities, it was found to give 200hp, whilst the British Beardmore unit of similar dimensions could produce little more than 160hp - further proof, if it were needed, that Porsche was an excellent all-round designer.

Porsche remained at Austro-Daimler until 1923, then went to Stuttgart to become the Technical Director of Daimler. His last celebrated design for Austro-Daimler was the Sascha, a small sportscar

which left its mark during the 1922 Targa Florio when Alfred Neubauer came in nineteenth overall and took victory in the Coppa Florio section. The paths of Porsche and Neubauer would cross again after the German driver joined the Mercedes team.

In 1926, Daimler became Daimler-Benz AG following the merger of Daimler and Benz - they had already been working together on technical and commercial fronts for a number of years - and from this date onwards the vehicles the company produced became universally known as Mercedes. Porsche stayed on until 1928, by which time the Mercedes had achieved a sporting reputation through various Porsche-designed racing and

Christian Werner on his way to victory on the 1924 Targa Florio. Porsche had vastly improved the Mercedes and, as an acknowledgement of his achievements, he was given an honorary doctorate by the Stuttgart Institute of Technology.

road cars, such as the SSK.

By now Porsche's reputation as a designer was unrivalled in Germany but, following a disagreement with the Daimler-Benz board, he decided to return home to Austria to join the Austrian Steyr company. The history of Steyr could be traced back to the early nineteenth century, although the car manufacturing side of the business was not founded until 1920. Unfortunately, the depression that followed the Wall Street Crash left this company in financial difficulties and, with a merger between Steyr and his old employers Austro-Daimler on the cards, Porsche resigned.

Although he was offered a number of positions within the industry, Porsche felt it was time to set up his own company and so with financial help from ex-colleague, Adolf Rosenberger (a driver for the Mercedes team), a design studio was established in Stuttgart in December 1930 and officially registered in the following April.

A team of engineers and designers was put together from the various firms with which Porsche had been involved; Porsche's son, Ferry, was also employed. Ferry Porsche was born on 19 September 1909, when his father was still heavily involved with the Austro-Daimler company. He was to be Ferdinand Porsche's only son and started driving from a very early age, carrying out the routine maintenance on the cars his father had built him from the age of ten. Ferry

was educated in Weiner-Neustadt and, later, in Stuttgart after Porsche's move to Daimler in 1923.

By 1928, Ferry Porsche had entered an apprenticeship with Bosch. After a year's thorough training, he followed his father to Steyr, where he trained in mechanical engineering, mathematics and technical drawing. Ferry Porsche inherited much of his father's natural flair for engineering and this talent was to give him a solid platform on which to build so that others would soon recognize him as a gifted engineer in his own right.

At this time Ferry was also becoming something of a racing driver, having driven for Wanderer and being involved with the testing of the Auto Union Grand Prix car. However, his father was to put an end to his competition days, saying: "He might get to like this sort of thing and want to become a racing driver, but his job is to design."

It is perhaps fortunate for today's motoring enthusiasts that Porsche did stop racing because pre-war it was a very dangerous sport indeed. Many people had been killed in their quest for speed, and the world could well have been

denied the genius of Dr. Ferry Porsche and, without him, the Porsche company would never have evolved. Anyway, at the time Ferry joined his father's design consultancy, he was twenty-one years old.

Naturally, in view of the financial climate, times were very hard for the fledgling business but a steady flow of consultancy work ensured the company's survival. From just thirteen employees in 1930, the number had risen to well over one hundred by the start of the Second World War. The list of companies that had approached Porsche is quite staggering: Steyr, Wanderer, Horch, Zundapp, Auto Union, Mathis, NSU, Morris, Citroën, Standard, Volvo, Triumph, ERA, Rochet-Schneider, Delaunay-Belleville, Austro-Fiat, Daimler-Benz and Volkswagen.

When Adolf Hitler was elected the new Chancellor of Germany, he was very supportive of German industry and financed the Mercedes-Benz and Auto Union racing programmes (Auto Union had been formed in 1932, and consisted of the old Audi, DKW, Horch and Wanderer companies now trading under one banner) to show the world how strong the German na-

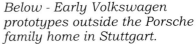

Porsche also designed the V16 Auto Union Grand Prix car, one of the vehicles that formed the basis of the Silver Arrows legend.

Below - Early Volkswagen prototypes outside the Porsche family home in Stuttgart.

provided the basis for the Porsche success story. The Volkswagen Beetle was a natural progression from former Porsche small car designs, the Type 12 (built for Zundapp) providing the basic mechanical layout and the body shape defined by the Erwin Komenda-styled Type 32 of 1933.

After a 1934 meeting, in which Hitler himself approved the plans for the people's car (*volkswagen*), Porsche set about building three prototypes by hand and these were completed behind the closed doors of the garage at his home in Stuttgart. The people's car was designed to meet some difficult criteria: it would have a one litre 26hp engine with a cruising speed of 100kph, very good fuel economy and a remarkably low selling price. A further thirty prototypes were built by Daimler-Benz while Porsche visited various factories in America and the Austin plant in England to gain modern ideas on mass-production.

Just as Hitler was passing the final plans for the Volkswagen, and after 1.8 million miles of testing with the prototypes, the Second World War broke out. The largest car factory in the world was then, for the duration of the war, mainly given over to the production of military vehicles based on the VW design. The Wolfsburg factory was badly damaged by Allied bombing so that, at the end of the war in Germany, the Volkswagen project could easily have died alongside

tion was when it came to technical innovation. It should be noted that Auto Union's V16 Grand Prix car was a Porsche design which was hugely successful in both racing and record breaking.

It is perhaps one of the later pre-war projects, the complete design of the Volkswagen (again funded by Hitler's Nazi Party), that

the fallen dictator, had not help come from an unexpected quarter.

Mention must be made at this stage of the three Type 64 Berlin-Rome racers. The race, due to take place in September 1939 and devised by Hitler's aides as a political statement to show the partnership of the German Nazi and Italian Fascist parties (and seen as the ideal launching platform for the new Volkswagen), was naturally cancelled at the outbreak of war. However, Porsche had built three lightweight streamlined coupes for the event, powered by VW flat-four engines tuned to give 40bhp. Ac-

cording to an article in *Classic Cars* in 1982, one was used by the American military and later broken up, another was used by Dr. Bodo Lafferentz of the German Labour Front, whilst the third was saved by the Austrian racing driver, Otto Mathé, who obtained it from Professor Porsche and used the car competitively with a good deal of postwar success. Based on the Beetle, the Type 64 was definitely the forerunner of the Porsche 356. Sadly, six years of global conflict would delay any further development. The Type 116, which was basically similar to the Type 64

except for its 1.5 litre Volkswagen power-unit, mounted in the mid-engined position, was also scuppered.

Professor Porsche (he was awarded the title of honorary Professor in 1940) was interrogated by the British and the American authorities following the war, being arrested at his family home in Zell Am See. He was released quickly and went to Renault where he was asked to suggest a number of modifications for their 4CV model. Whilst there, Porsche and his son-in-law, Anton Piech, were arrested and imprisoned by the French on war

One of the Porsche Berlin-Rome racers, seen here competing in 1952 with Otto Mathé at the wheel. Truly the forerunner of the Porsche 356.

Professor Porsche and his son, Ferry. Ferry Porsche had been brought up around cars, so it came as no surprise that the motor industry was his chosen profession.

criminal charges, with a ransom of one million francs.

Ferry Porsche had also been imprisoned for a short time, but Louise Piech had managed to negotiate the release of her brother. However, with the Porsche offices in Stuttgart occupied by the United States Army, Ferry Porsche had little chance of raising the ransom money. By an amazing stroke of luck, Porsche was approached by Carlo Abarth (the famous engine tuner) and his partner, Piero Dusio, a rich Italian industrialist and motoring enthusiast who, among other things, wanted to build a

Grand Prix car.

The Cisitalia, as it was known, drew heavily on the Auto Union of the 1930s, and was very complex. It was powered by a rear-mounted 1.5 litre flat-twelve, with a dohc set-up on each bank of cylinders and twin super-chargers. An ingenious four-wheel drive system was devised for the Type 360, to make the most of the car's 350hp and over 200mph performance.

The Cisitalia project was sadly destined to fail, as escalating development costs put a successful car out of the reach of even Dusio's wealth. However, it did provide Ferry Porsche with enough money to release his father from the French prison. After some negotiations, the Professor was allowed back to Austria in August 1947, and was later cleared of all the charges levelled against him.

In the meantime, the Volkswagen factory had been taken out of the hands of the Germans. However, instead of letting the Volkswagen project die, its management

Professor Ferdinand Porsche, 1875-1951.

was taken over by British officials. After a slow start getting production underway in less than ideal conditions, the Volkswagen Beetle became one of the most successful cars ever built, if numbers alone are anything to go by.

Professor Ferdinand Porsche died on 30 January 1951, having suffered a stroke a couple of months earlier. His health had never been the same following his imprisonment in France, but at least he was able to see his son develop a new car bearing the family name and the fruition of his ideas for a people's car in the shape of the successful VW Beetle.

Porsche's road car, based on the Volkswagen Beetle, would eventually become known as the 356. This car forms the core subject of this book, and was the foundation stone of the Porsche legend. The proof of Porsche's enduring worldwide appeal is probably best summed up by the Japanese *Car Magazine* which, in 1995, compiled their all-time top ten of sportscars. They voted the 356 range in at number four, while the 911 range was declared number one. In the pages that follow, I hope to establish why the Porsche 356 remains so universally popular.

PORSCHE 356

2

THE FIRST PORSCHE

With the Allies advancing on Stuttgart in 1944 the major players in the Porsche team were sent to Gmünd in Austria. This area, near Spittal and close to the Italian border, was chosen because of its freedom from bombing raids. The Gmünd site consisted of one large wooden building (formally a sawmill) and a small office constructed from the same material. It would later become the birthplace of the first Porsche car to bear its designer's name.

After the war, until the Cisitalia project came about, money was obtained through the servicing and repair of ex-Army Volkswagens and, in addition, the design and manufacture of agricultural equipment. The Porsche family business was remarkably successful given the financial climate of the time. The Cisitalia contract was signed during February 1947 and, within a few months, gave Ferry Porsche enough cash to free his father from the French prison.

It also led to a visit by Ferry Porsche and Karl Rabe to the

The key staff at Gmünd (from left to right): Karl Rabe, Erwin Komenda and Ferry Porsche.

Porsche Number One, the first road car to bear the family name.

Cisitalia works in Italy. Some people, such as ex-employee Rodolfo Hruska, say it was the visit to Cisitalia (at the time they were building some simple but beautiful sports cars based on Fiat mechanicals) that inspired Porsche to build the 356. However, Ferry Porsche had had a small sports car in mind for years, so this doesn't seem all that likely - perhaps the word "prompted" would be more correct than "inspired"?

Karl Rabe, incidentally, had been Professor Porsche's protégé at Austro-Daimler and was one of the first key members of the Porsche design bureau when it opened in Stuttgart. He would be Porsche's Chief Engineer until 1966, so his career spans the whole of the 356's development.

In any case, Ferry Porsche decided that his small company should construct a motor car based around Volkswagen components. Allocated the Porsche design number Type 356, the first drawing was dated 17 July 1947, just one month after the project was instigated.

The first chassis (number 356-001) was completed in March 1948 and was duly tested by Ferry and Eberan von Eberhorst (of Auto Union design fame) on the Katschberg Pass and the Grossglockner toll road: the latter being the venue for the first Volkswagen demonstrations. With the prototype open body (built by Friedrich Weber) fitted in late-May,

Other members of staff at Gmünd in 1948. The back row (left to right) has Paul Ernst, Leopold Schmid, Ewald Mozelt, Richard Hetmann and Hans Chabek; seated are Wilhelm Gasteig, Herr Kral (Komenda's assistant), Herr Herzog and Wolfgang Eyb.

the Porsche was clocked at 84mph.

The spaceframe chassis on the first car was very well designed, allowing a large door opening on each side to reveal the three-abreast seating arrangement. Although the car required very little tooling to build - perfect for a prototype - construction was too labour-intensive for cost-effective series production.

The first car's body design, drawn up by Erwin Komenda with help from Ferry Porsche, was very advanced. Built by Porsche's master panel beater, Friedrich Weber (ex-Austro-Daimler), it was beautifully smooth - even the door handles were flush with the body to cut wind resistance (the square "POR-SCHE" lettering which featured on their original car's nose has been retained as a trademark to this day). It was light, too, the whole car weighing in at less than 1340lbs.

The engine was a fairly standard 1131cc Volkswagen unit mounted back to front, with a single downdraught carburettor (twin carburettors were subsequently fitted) and a higher compression ratio (increased to 7:1 despite the poor quality of the fuel then available). The heads, camshafts and so on were also suitably modified to give more power; whereas a standard Volkswagen unit gave 25bhp, the first Porsche engine (number 356-2-034969) gave 40bhp.

Although the engine position gave good weight distribution and therefore good handling, unfortu-

nately, it took up too much space to allow for more than two seats within the original 82.7 inch wheelbase. Engine access was difficult and the gearbox had to be modified to avoid having four reverse and one forward gears. The engine's position also caused problems with rear suspension location, prompting Porsche to change the trailing arms into leading arms. This strange rear suspension set-up caused the tube carrying the torsion bars to give way during a road test (the Volkswagen had the trailing arms located on the strong centre section instead of the weaker rear), but at least the car limped home after receiving some temporary strengthening.

Porsche Number One passed its statutory Austrian test on 8 June and, during the same month, was taken to the European Grand Prix in Switzerland to allow journalists to try the car. A deliberately soft ride was built into the suspension set-up, as Dr. Porsche believed that "the wheels have to work if they are going to stick to the road." Max Troesch, who wrote for *Motor* at the time, was impressed and made note of the "remarkable roadholding ... and very light, ac-

curate steering."

Automobil Revue did the first road test of the Porsche in their July 1948 issue, noting it had the "handling of a modern car and good comfort." They summed up their good opinion of the vehicle by saying: "This is how we imagine modern road motoring to be ..."

It was also at this meeting that Porsche met Rupprecht von Senger, who was particularly enthusiastic - this Swiss businessman would be a very useful contact later on. Other encouraging news had come on 20 June 1948, when the Reichsmark was replaced by the Deutschmark. Germany now had a free market economy, making it much easier to trade. Mindful of his eventual intention to return to Germany and satisfied with the response his little machine received, Porsche felt sure that a limited production run would be a safe bet.

The biggest problem for any would-be car manufacturer in Austria in the immediate postwar years was the supply of components. For the prototype, most of the electrical equipment was bought from Swiss companies and the spark plugs were smuggled across the border from the German Bosch works.

Ferry Porsche and his father oversee the building of the chassis for the first coupé.

There was also a great shortage of metal and, indeed, in the quiet Gmünd area, a lack of suitable skilled workers.

Herbert Kaes, Professor Porsche's nephew, entered a local race in Innsbruck on 11 July 1948 and won a Class victory. In September, however, Porsche Number One was sold to a Swiss customer (despite the trading restrictions in force at the time) in order to obtain some much-needed foreign currency - 7000 Swiss Francs - although the car was bought back by the factory in 1958.

This customer was Rupprecht von Senger of Zurich, whom Porsche had met in Berne at the Grand Prix. Von Senger's partner, Bernhard Blank, (who ran an advertising agency at the time of meeting Porsche) agreed to buy the next four cars and formed a car dealership called AMAG for distributing

Porsches. This new concern also proved to be very helpful in getting supplies from Wolfsburg to Gmünd, dealing in Swiss Francs and having the freedom to travel. The Swiss also supplied sheet aluminium in order for body production to continue at Gmünd.

The Second Prototype

From the second car onwards, the engine position reverted to the traditional Volkswagen layout (*ie* with the gearbox and transaxle in front of the engine) allowing Porsche to make the car a true 2+2. Once again braking, steering and independent torsion bar suspension components came directly from Wolfsburg. A sheet steel platform chassis was used, making series production easier.

This was the first coupé, and was completed in late August 1948. By all accounts, the production

road cars were always intended to be Grand Tourers as open cars were thought to be not really suitable for central European winters - the open prototype was produced simply because it was easier to build and could therefore be used to test public reaction quicker.

The aerodynamics of the 356 coupé were very good (a Cd figure of 0.29 has been quoted) and, allied to the lack of openings at the front and the seamless construction of the body, this meant the Porsche was capable of some very high speeds for such a small-engined car. The streamlined shape also helped fuel consumption: around 30mpg could be expected whatever the driving conditions.

Announced during late Summer 1948, the car's public debut was scheduled for the Geneva Show in 1949. In the first brochure, printed in German, English and

The modified Volkswagen engine, as fitted to the first coupé.

Below - The completed prototype Porsche coupé with the Number One Roadster behind. The coupé has already picked up a dent on the nose during testing.

French, the Porsche 356 was shown in both open and closed form. Engine size was listed at 1131cc, though it would not be long before

Experiments were carried out with tufts of wool taped to the body to gauge air flow.

Below - The production process at Gmünd was a little primitive ...

design a direct competitor to the Beetle. In return, Volkswagen could use any Porsche patents free-of-charge for a royalty of 5DM on each

a 1086cc capacity (73.5 x 64mm) was chosen, allowing the cars to compete in the 1100cc Class at International level. The first Porsche brochure claimed a top speed of 87mph and 0-60 in a fraction over 7 seconds - both perhaps a little hopeful!

In the meantime, in mid September 1948, Porsche sealed a deal with Volkswagen securing the supply of parts providing Porsche didn't car built. Porsche were also entitled to use the Volkswagen service network and sell their cars through Volkswagen dealers.

The Gmünd cars were completely hand-built, their aluminium

The interior of a Gmünd-built cabriolet of 1949; note the fascinating dashboard design. Some of these early cars had individual seats, others a bench seat.

bodies being beaten into shape as there simply wasn't the money available to tool up. Around five cars a month were completed from the final months of 1948 onwards.

As mentioned earlier, drophead versions of the 356 were listed in the first catalogue, and the early examples came courtesy of Beutler in Switzerland, which started build-

ing a total of six open bodies for Porsche during the Autumn of 1948 (one is known to survive). The Beutler Brothers business was established shortly after the war by

Fritz and Ernst Beutler in Dürrenast near Thun, Ernst having previously worked at Graber.

The Beutler drophead coupé had an aluminium body and fully retractable hood. It first appeared at the Geneva Show in March 1949 alongside a yellow coupé - it was the first international exhibition for Porsche. The last Beutler dhc was delivered to Bernhard Blank in August 1949.

The Geneva Show, which opened on 17 March, was a great success for Porsche, attracting a lot of business. Apart from Switzerland, Austria and Germany, other early orders came from customers in Holland, Sweden, and Portugal - the latter offered to trade shiploads of sardines for fifteen vehicles! One of the first customers was a cousin of King Farouk of Egypt - Prince Abd el Moneim.

Reutter's prototype of March 1950. The people in the photograph are as follows (from the left): Karl Schmidt, Hugo Heiner, Alfred Haag, Alfred Waibel, Gustav Wolfe, Hans Klauser, Herbert Linge, Karl Kirn, Eberhard Storz and Alfred Braunschweiger.

Stuttgart-built Porsches

As orders flooded in, it was obvious that the Gmünd works would soon outlive their usefulness. The Mayor of Stuttgart was approached in mid-1949 to request a return to that city. With the Mayor's blessing, the Porsche family home in Feuerbacher Beg was adopted as the new headquarters until the original works could be occupied

again. Nonetheless, it was soon realised that production would not be practical in such a confined area.

In the meantime, in May 1949, Porsche Salzburg was formed. Run by Louise Piech (Ferry Porsche's sister), this company handled Volkswagen sales as well as dealing with the new Porsche car and

later the Gmünd operation was moved there (eventually it would become the headquarters for Volkswagen in Austria). To aid engine performance, a special cylinder head, produced by Karl Schmidt of Neckarsulm, was fitted to the 356 from November 1949.

It was obvious that if production was to continue, pressed steel

This photograph was taken in 1951 and shows a rarely seen aspect of production at Reutter!

would have to be considered for the bodywork because it was both cheaper to use and easier to work with. Dealers were approached to gauge their reaction to a steel-bodied car, and 37 were pre-sold before the first Stuttgart-built 356 was completed.

Serious production began early in 1950 when the firm moved back to the Zuffenhausen area of Stuttgart. However, as the Porsche site was still being used by the American military as a motor pool, the factory belonging to Porsche's neighbours - the Reutter body works - was used first. In November 1949 Reutter had been given the contract to build the bodies for Porsche and so provided a 5400 square foot workspace in their factory to the returning firm for 500DM a month.

The Berlin Airlift, which started in 1948, suggested a world ill at ease following the postwar agreements drawn up at Potsdam and Yalta, but what had become West Germany in May 1949 was, in fact,

The cabriolet and coupé entered on the Midnight Sun Rally of 1950. Behind the cars (from the left) are: Prince Joachim zu Fürstenberg, Ferry Porsche, Count Berckheim, Prince Günther zu Fürstenberg and Count Günther zu Hardenberg. The 1.1 litre coupé won its Class. (The marks on the photo show how it was to be retouched for publicity use).

A delightful period scene showing a coupé from 1950/51: the nose and roofline differed from those of the Gmünd cars, as did the interior trim. The steel-bodied cars were heavier, too.

and lower roofline than their steel-bodied counterparts and a slightly different nose. The interior trim was changed, and swivelling quarterlights were a feature, strangely, not carried over to the steel-bodied machines built in the Stuttgart works until much later on. The Gmünd cars also featured Lockheed front brakes, whereas the Stuttgart models used standard Volkswagen fare.

According to Ferry Porsche, 46 cars were built at Gmünd between 8 June 1948 and 20 March 1951 (when the site was finally vacated). However, figures vary wildly between sources, most quoting 50 or 51 vehicles. If one is to take Mr. Porsche's total - for there can surely be none better - maybe it doesn't include the Number One prototype and the four machines kept back for racing? The 50 quote wouldn't include the Number One prototype, while the 51 total would - maybe!

Porsche had an impressive list of famous customers which helped sales abroad. Of the Gmünd cars, no less than 12 went to Switzerland, and 15 went to Sweden through Scania-Vabis. Some of the Gmünd cars were finished by Austro-Tatra of Vienna and also by Keibl (who would later body the Denzel). Competition success was also a strong selling point.

The first Porsche 356 manufactured in Stuttgart was later written-off in a high-speed accident when being driven by engine spe-

quite stable. Theodor Heuss was voted in as the first President of the Federal Republic in September of that year and was re-elected for a second term in 1954. Marshall Aid from America helped West Germany recover quickly from the hardship and shortages of the immediate postwar years.

The 1950 steel-bodied car was offered at 10,200DM in its native country, the first one being completed on 6 April 1950 as a light grey coupé named the *Windhund* (German for greyhound). To put the price into perspective, at the same time the Volkswagen Beetle was priced at 4800DM.

There were a number of subtle differences between the Stuttgart cars and the Gmünd cars. The Gmünd alloy cars had a narrower

Right - The first Reutter prototype was not symmetrical, but, as will be seen in this photograph taken at the 1950 Paris Salon the production models were perfect. On the left is the Windhund, *the first car to leave the Stuttgart works, and later became Ferry Porsche's personal car.*

cialist Rolf Wutherich. Several years later, Wutherich was lucky to survive an even more serious accident - he was James Dean's passenger when the young star crashed in his Porsche Spyder.

A Start in Motorsport
The first International competition entry came in June 1950, when two alloy-bodied cars were sent to Sweden to take part in the Rally of the Midnight Sun. Prince Joachim zu Fürstenberg and Count Konstantin Berckheim won their Class in a 1086cc coupé, while Countess Cecilia Koskull, a private entry, took the Ladies Prize in her Gmünd coupé; Porsche took another Class win in 1951. It is interesting to note that the works always used the alloy Gmünd coupés, as they were lighter than the Stuttgart-built machines.

At the end of July 1950, Otto Mathé put in an impressive performance to win his Class in the Austrian Alpine Rally; another Class win came in the Interlaken Rally for Count von der Mühle-Eckart and Rudolph Sauerwein.

Cornering quickly became an art form for the enthusiastic 356 driver, but if the limit was exceeded, the car could flip over onto its roof. That said, if the 356 had been a poor car in the handling department, it would never have been as successful as it was. When the correct technique for fast cornering was mastered (*wischen* or wiping as it was called), the car became

a great source of enjoyment and the traction was very good in almost all conditions, even snow. Richard von Frankenberg once said: "When one has understood this controlled wiping motion, better still, when its mastery has become part of your blood, then Porsche driving becomes enormous fun!"

The Loss of Professor Porsche
At the 1950 Paris Show, where the firm made a big thing of the Porsche name being involved in the industry for fifty years, an ailing Ferdinand Porsche held talks with Max Hoffman and others to try and get the 356 into America. In November, he visited the Wolfsburg factory to pay what was to be his first, and only, visit to the Volkswagen works.

Following his term in prison, Professor Porsche lacked the drive and enthusiasm of pre-war days; in fact, he had been severely weakened by the whole experience. By the end of 1950, he was gravely ill and never really recovered from a stroke. In January 1951, the great man died.

Of course, Professor Porsche had wanted to build a Volkswagen sports car before the war, but the idea had been scuppered by the Labour Front; after all, in a Socialist environment, why should there be elitist drivers with faster machines? In the end, the 356 would be the only Porsche-badged sports cars that the Professor was involved with and, even then, the model was

more to do with his son.

At Professor Porsche's funeral, the German Minister of Transport said: "Ferdinand Porsche was the last of the great designers whose name was famous all over the world. He belonged to the likes of Daimler, Bugatti and Lancia whose names denote the make of motor car. Today's designers remain anonymous, their names being known only to their colleagues in the same line."

Expansion of the Business
In December 1950, a small design and management office near the Reutter works was purchased for 19,000DM and soon a racing shop was attached with just enough room for two cars and four mechanics. Ferry Porsche, when asked about plans for the future in an interview for *Road & Track* magazine in 1950, replied: "The Porsche car is a handmade special car. The Porsche firm is first and foremost a design and consulting engineering firm. For this reason, they are not particularly interested in raising their production, since they want to keep on making fine handmade cars." The reality, of course, was that the consultancy work was drying-up.

Perhaps the biggest single factor in Porsche's expansion was the American market. In October 1950, Max Hoffman had travelled to the Paris Show to negotiate possible terms as a Porsche distributor for America. At that time, Ferry Porsche thought the American market

would take around five cars a year, but Hoffman had other ideas, and told him to expect five cars a week. Naturally, Hoffman was appointed as the East Coast Porsche agent for the USA!

Maximillian Hoffman was born in Vienna, and raced motorcycles in his younger days before becoming a car importer in his native country. When he moved to America, he made use of his many contacts and began selling foreign cars from his Park Avenue showroom in New York.

Three 356s were imported in the Autumn of 1950: two were sold to Briggs Cunningham and one Hoffman kept for himself. At $4500 the Porsche was more expensive than a Cadillac convertible coupé, while a Jaguar XK120 could be bought for less than $4000. But Hoffman regarded the Porsche as "a German automotive jewel" and,

A Porsche 356 cabriolet from early 1951. Note the vee-windscreen and how the bumper is attached to the body. Most cabriolet bodies were built by Glaser of Ullesricht, while the hoods were constructed by Reutter or Heuer.

Below - Le Mans 1951, with the Veuillet/Mouche car in the pits on one of its routine stops.

in the event, sold thirty two cars in 1951.

In 1950, the Stuttgart concern had a staff of 108, with planned production of around ten cars per month. In the event, this target was easily doubled, and nearly 300 Porsche 356s were built in the year (actually 298). By 1951, the staff had increased to 214 and between them they constructed a total of 1103 cars, 25 per cent of which were exported. The 500th German-built 356 was driven out of the works on 21 March 1951 by Hans Klauser, the Personnel Manager, while on 28 August, the 1000th 356 left the factory.

New Engines

By March 1951, 1.3 litre (1283cc Type 506) engines were available and, by now, Porsche's own brakes (supplied by Ate, Lockheed's

German agents) were fitted; 'crash' gearboxes were still sourced from Volkswagen at this stage. The more refined 1300 had been made possible by Mahle, the piston manufacturers, who were responsible for the pioneering technique of coating aluminium with thousands of regularly-spaced tiny chrome dots. The chrome was harder wearing, and used in this way produced less friction and dispersed heat quicker. Porsche used the process on cylinder bores.

The 1300 engine was actually 12lb lighter than its 1100 counterpart, and gave 44bhp. Porsche power was always quoted in DIN bhp (which equates roughly to the power available at the wheels), so to British and American drivers (who are used to quotes referring to flywheel power, and often exaggerated at that), performance felt amazingly lively for such a low-powered car.

The 1500 (1488cc Type 527) became available in October 1951, although the Type 369 1100 unit continued well into 1954. The 1500 needed a Hirth roller bearing crankshaft, as the clearance between the crankshaft and camshaft wasn't enough to just increase the stroke. The crank developed by Albert Hirth allowed the use of a one-piece con-rod that didn't have big end bolts - it gave just enough space. The 1500 initially gave 55bhp, increased later to 60bhp and, with a special cam, to 70bhp.

Great care was taken in the assembly of the 356. For example each engine was built by one fitter and then initialled. The gearbox and transaxle were dealt with in a similar fashion; the steering box was set up on a special rig and moved from lock-to-lock for a whole day to ensure perfect movement and, finally, each car received a 60-mile road test after completion.

Success in Motorsport 1951
Following a request from Charles Faroux, one of the organisers of the 1951 Le Mans 24-hour Race (and also one of the people who secured Professor Porsche's release from prison), Porsche promised to send two cars to the classic event.

Sadly, only one car representing the marque made it to the line as the other was destroyed during practice and, due to earlier mishaps, there was no spare machine.

Prototype four-seater Porsche, given the Type 530 designation. A cabriolet was also built.

The car at Le Mans was a 356SL (SL meaning Super Lightweight); engines were tuned to 46bhp and aluminium panels were added beneath the cars to aid aerodynamics. In addition, the wheels were covered over and there were larger fuel tanks.

The team manager for the event was Paul von Guilleaume, who would later drive Porsches in competition. Auguste Veuillet and Edmond Mouche, who had driven a Delage together in 1949, took the car to 20th overall and first in Class, despite the car being stuck in third gear for the last 200 miles.

This was to be the first of Porsche's appearances at the Sarthe circuit, but it certainly wouldn't be the last, and major success was only a few years away. In fact, at the time of writing, the Stuttgart company held the record for the most outright victories at Le Mans.

For the 1951 Baden-Baden Rally, there were two factory-entered cars but, sadly, after sixteen hours of hard driving on the Autobahn their tyres gave way, throwing their treads. If nothing else, the event proved that the 1300cc Porsches were the fastest production cars in Germany at that time.

On the international calendar, the Liège-Rome-Liège Rally (or Marathon de la Route) of August 1951 was a great success for Porsche. The 1100cc car with Huschke von Hanstein and Petermax Müller came second in Class, while the 1500cc car of Paul von Guillaume and Count von der Mühle came first in Class and third overall. This was the first time that the 1500 engine was used - as was announced to the public shortly after - but not before it was given one further test.

In September, a five-man team with a 1.1 litre and 1.5 litre coupé plus a 1.5 litre Glockler machine (see Chapter 3) were sent to Montléry. Between them they set 17 new Class records, with the 1.5 litre coupé attaining a World Record of 152.34kph over 72 hours. To reinforce the worth of the new 1.5 litre engine, the Montlhéry record car was shown at the 1951 Paris Salon - still covered in road dirt!

Porsche Specials

The Type 530 of 1951 was a 356 with a longer 2400mm (94.5 inch) wheelbase to allow for four seats. A coupé and convertible model were made, both with a new tail line and 1.5 litre engines. After extensive testing, the official line was that the cars weren't put into production for marketing reasons, although it is more likely that the extra costs involved in manufacturing the four-seaters killed off the project.

Wolfgang Denzel, an Austrian engineer and motoring enthusiast, built a four-seater sports car based on Volkswagen parts in 1948. Shortly after, Denzel and Hubert Stroinigg won the Austrian Alpine

This is what happened to most America Roadsters. Here's John von Neumann pushing hard in a race at Reno in 1953.

for Volkswagen were interesting in that the resultant machines were so close to the Porsche. Started in 1952, both cars used standard Volkswagen parts, and were presumably instigated as a possible replacement for the Beetle. However, after they were presented to the Board at Wolfsburg they were ordered to be scrapped.

Another project that came to nothing was the design of an American-style Volkswagen-type vehicle for Studebaker. Set up by Hoffman, the deal was sealed in May 1952 and the resultant four-door saloon with an air- or water-cooled engine was very elegant. Sadly, Studebaker ran into financial troubles, bringing the development of the Type 542 to an end.

The America Roadster

Johnny von Neumann bought one of the last Gmünd coupés and converted it into a lightweight racing roadster. With its aero-screen in place, it was seen on American race tracks until 1953 and it's not hard to see why it is said that von Neumann's car inspired the Speedster design. However, there was another model which may have played a role ...

Cars were not selling as quickly as hoped for by Hoffman in the USA. Price was a factor and, although he loved the engineering, Hoffman wasn't all that keen on the Porsche's shape. Later, he and Porsche went to the American artist Coby Whitmore who sketched

Rally in their glassfibre-bodied car. In addition, the Coupe des Alpes was gained in 1954 with Denzel himself at the wheel and, in 1956, with M. Lauga driving.

After his initial success, Denzel was flooded with orders for replicas. In 1951, he moved away from the Volkswagen chassis to one built from welded tubular steel, making the car even lighter and, by 1952, the glassfibre body had been re-placed by a hand-beaten aluminium body. The Denzel car was available as a coupé, roadster (with or without hardtop) or as a convertible and with various engine options - usually Porsche. In certain export markets, such as North America, the car was known as the "WD" but, after around 350 vehicles had been produced, the Denzel was discontinued in 1959.

The Type 534 and 555 projects

Interior of the America Roadster production model.

Below - Von de Kaart and Swaters on the 1952 Monte Carlo Rally. Note the higher mounting of the headlights for the event.

out something a little nearer Hoffman's tastes and, indeed, what he thought the Americans wanted. The resultant vehicle was the Type 540, better known in Porsche circles as the "America Roadster."

The America Roadster was based on the 356 cabriolet floorpan but, in view of its expected use on the tracks, it was endowed with extra strengthening. Aluminium body panels by Heuer of Weiden, a spartan cockpit, and detachable side windows were used to save weight - the whole vehicle weighed only 1575lb. Fitted with a 70bhp 1.5 litre Porsche unit, this car was very quick indeed.

Built from April 1952, the America Roadster was soon being put to use in competition. Campaigned by the likes of Briggs Cunningham, Jack McAfee, John von Neumann, John Bentley and Phil Walters, it established itself in the 1500cc Class in American racing despite only sixteen having been built. In one test, a 0-60 time of 9.3 seconds was recorded, with a top speed of 110mph. Although the car was really only intended for the American market, one was raced in Germany by Kurt Zeller.

Competition in 1952

Mention must be made of an event held on 6 April 1952 called the Dieburg Triangle Race. Really a race for motorcycles, it included a Production Sportscar Race for vehicles with engine capacities of up to 1100cc. This was the start of

Mme *Largeot and* Mme *Sigrand with their 1300 coupé. They gained the Ladies Prize on the 1952 Rallye AC du Nord.*

Below - The 356SL Porsche, as used at Le Mans in 1951, 1952 and 1953. By the car, Mlle *Thirion, Belgium's fastest lady driver.*

1500 coupé. Berckheim was quite lucky to make it to Brescia as during testing he was nearly arrested in Germany for speeding!

In the event, Johnny Lurani and Constantin Berckheim won the 1500cc GT Class despite being stuck in third gear for the last part of the race and were followed home by two other Porsches. The Lurani 356 had averaged 65.7mph for the course, against 80.4mph for the winning Ferrari. The Porsche of Metternich/Einseidel won the 1100cc Sports Class, averaging 61.5mph.

At Le Mans, Veuillet and Mouche again won their 1100cc Class, coming 11th overall; their average speed went up from 73.54 to 76.51mph. Two other 356s were entered by the works, but Huschke von Hanstein's car retired in the sixth hour and the other was disqualified.

In the Liège-Rome-Liège Rally (Marathon de la Route), Porsche had a truly stunning result. From three works cars and a number of private entries, Helmut Polensky and Walter Schlütter won the event outright with their 1.5 litre 356. Porsche's finished first, third, fourth, ninth and tenth and, deservedly, took the marque Team Prize.

The "Carrera Panamericana" series of races started in 1950 and was instigated to celebrate the opening of the Pan-American highway, planned to run all the way from Alaska to Tierra del Fuego. A

a new series, with the Nürburgring races being especially popular because the limit was 1500cc. Max Nathan won the first event at the Nürburgring, but another driver to come through these ranks was a certain Hans Herrmann.

Porsche's first entry on the Mille Miglia came in 1952. On 4 May, one works car (a Gmünd coupé because it was over 200lb lighter than a steel-bodied 356) lined up at the start alongside three private entries - Count Metternich/Count Einseidel and R. von Frankenberg/ H. U. Wieselmann had 1100s with hotter Fuhrmann cam (48 instead of 46bhp). Helmut Polensky had a

number of Continental manufacturers grasped the opportunity to prove their wares in the Mexican race (it would have been impossible to stage such a fast and dangerous event in the States), which gained excellent coverage in the world's biggest market for sports cars - America.

Porsche were represented by private entries in 1952 but, in the following year, the factory sent a team of works' cars. Paul Alfons von Metternich in a 356 Super featured in the top ten of two stages, finishing ninth on the Parral-Chihuahua leg and eighth on the final run from Chihuahua to Ciudad Juarez. This was enough for him to secure eighth overall in the Sport Class.

Thirion on the 1952 Tour de France. The event was won by a DB Panhard.

Production Changes

The racing experience gained by Porsche in their early years gave rise to a number of modifications to their road cars. Perhaps the most important of all, after numerous problems with the old Volkswagen unit, was the introduction of a better gearbox (Type 519). The Porsche servo-assisted synchromesh system, designed by Leopold Schmid, had first been seen on the Cisitalia Grand Prix car but it would soon be adopted on the 356 production models. Introduced to the public at the 1952 Paris Salon, the new transmission was distinguishable from the cockpit by the longer and cranked gearlever.

In September 1952, by changing the size and position of the camshaft and modifying the big ends, the 1500 was now built using plain bearings. Giving 55bhp, the Type 546 engine was a more refined unit (as John Bolster put it: "the Super is neither so flexible nor so quiet as the less highly-developed version") and the cars fitted with it became known as the *damen*

The Porsches entered for the 1952 Carrera Panamericana. The coupé was crewed by Count Berckheim and Herbert Linge, while the cabriolet was driven by Von Metternich. The latter was the best finisher, coming eighth in the Sport Class (the gearbox failed on the coupé).

The 1953 model year chassis, with new engine, exhaust pipes, gearbox, wheels and steering wheel design. Note the new Porsche badge in the centre of the steering wheel.

Production at Zuffenhausen at the end of 1952. Note the new bumper arrangement and rear lights on the cars nearest the camera, and also the America Roadster on the line (to the left).

(lady) model. Roller bearing engines giving 70bhp became available from the Paris Salon onwards, these being known as the 1500 Super or, internally, Type 528.

Super engines benefited from bigger carburettors and ports, a higher compression ratio, a different exhaust system with better gas flow and a crankshaft running on roller bearings: the latter again being built up by Hirth. A Porsche badge, drawn up by Ferry on Hoffman's suggestion, was used from October 1952. It featured the crest of Baden-Württemburg with the Stuttgart coat-of-arms super-imposed upon it - the badge continues unchanged to this day.

Other important revisions, carried out during the early part of

36

An early 356 about to tackle one of the night stages of the 1953 Monte Carlo Rally.

Below - The 356 of Engel and Von Hoesch. Wearing a stoneguard for most of the event, it was taken off for the prize-giving, as the pairing took second place in the 1500cc Class of the 1953 Monte Carlo Rally. The event was won by Maurice Gatsonides in a Ford Zephyr.

1952, included the dropping of the old two-piece windscreen in April (it had been too costly to tool up for one-piece glass before) although the distinct V-shape was retained until 1955. New instruments were used and there were new ventilated steel wheels over bigger and better brakes. Stronger bumpers were also a feature, the latter now moved further away from the body.

The original Porsche factory in Stuttgart was supposed to have been handed back in September 1950 but, due to the alert caused by the Korean War, the American authorities held on to it. With no sign of the old factory being returned, at least not in the near future, another factory was built in 1952, next door to Reutter. By November 1952, the first cars were starting to roll out of *Werk II*. During 1952, with a staff of 332, a total of 1303 Porsche cars were built.

Competition in 1953

Huschke von Hanstein (born in 1911) had won the 1940 Mille Miglia for BMW and, having taken on the Public Relations side of Porsche in 1951, he also became the Racing Manager in 1953. The 1953 Mille Miglia was again dominated by Ferrari, but there were Class wins for Porsche in both the 1300cc Sports (Von Hoesch/Engel), and the 1500cc Sports category (Herrmann/Bauer). Von Hoesch and Engel also won the 1300cc Production Sports Class of the Nürburgring 1000km Race (a

Porsche took the 1500cc Class in that event as well) later in the year.

At Le Mans, two of the new 550 models with enclosed cockpits were entered by the works. One was driven by Richard von Frankenberg and Paul Frere (15th and first in Class) and the other was handled by Herrmann and H. Glockler (16th). The works' 356SL was again placed in the hands of Veuillet (although Müller was his partner on this occasion), but retired just six hours from the end. A 1.5 litre 356 privately-entered and driven by Gonzague Olivier was forced to pull out through engine trouble at around the same time.

In the French Alpine Rally, a number of Porsche drivers came away with the coveted Coupé des Alpes: Sauerwein, Zeller, Von

Otto Mathé awaiting his turn at the startline of the 1953 Freiburg-Schauinsland hillclimb.

Left - A privately-entered Porsche 356 on the 1953 Rallye Tirol.

English actress, Jacqueline Evans, with her 356; she was out of the Carrera Panamericana after the first leg. Fortunately, other Porsches did better.

Hoesch, Bulto-Marques, De Carlat and Polensky. Helmut Polensky was awarded the first European Rally Championship at the end of the season, although he had also driven a Fiat and Lancia during 1953.

The Carrera Panamericana of 1953 was again held in November and the under-1600cc Sport cat-

A Gmünd coupé at the end of its 1953 Carrera Panamericana. The car, driven by Guillermo Suhr, was one of four Porsches in the "Los Caminos" team from Guatemala. The other cars included two 550 models and a production 356 coupé.

egory was this time totally dominated by the Porsche marque. Karl Kling, who had won the event in 1952 for Mercedes-Benz, had been arrested and taken to Ellis Island. Apparently the authorities thought he was another Kling who was wanted on war crime charges, but fortunately the mistake was recognised and he was released three days later.

The race went better, and Porsche won five of the eight stages to take a one-two in Class: Jose Herrarte Ariano driving the 550 secured first place, while Fernando Segura took a 356 Super into second. In the general classification, the Porsches were awarded 32nd and 33rd overall, some six hours or so down on Fangio's winning Lancia.

It was the first appearance for the Porsche works on the opposite side of the Atlantic - much of the finance needed for the expedition had come from Max Hoffman who saw it as an investment in advertising. Hoffman was indeed a very shrewd man: the resultant publicity paid off handsomely and America

took 141 cars in 1952, but no less than 573 in 1953!

Press Reaction 1953

Styling is always a matter of personal taste. Max Hoffman had stated that he wasn't all that keen on the shape of the 356, but *Auto Motor und Sport* felt quite differently and said: "The fact is that the Porsche, all other considerations apart, is the most beautiful series-built car in the world today."

The 356's handling also gained mixed reactions, although some people were basing their opinions on theory rather than fact. Indeed, one would expect oversteer with the 356 layout, but it is to what extent that matters. Dr. Porsche once said, "It does not matter where the engine is located, as long as it is light." The average 356 power-unit of 1953 weighed in at only 160lbs, with front to rear dry weight distribution being approximately 45/55 per cent.

Maurice Gatsonides, testing a 1500 Super coupé for *Autosport* in June 1953 noted: "As soon as one

is accustomed to this very direct steering, it is real pleasure to steer the car with two fingers at 100 m.p.h. Neither is driving tiring, for the engine is very quiet. Up to speeds of 80 m.p.h. conversation is possible without raising one's voice in the slightest degree. Summing up briefly, the Porsche 1500 Super is a very remarkable sports car and, in the hands of a good driver, is a force to reckon with in competitions."

John Bolster added: "In practice, the Porsche does oversteer in quite a big way, but the experienced driver, having entered a corner at speed, allows the steering to unwind as the turn is negotiated, which can be a smooth and effortless operation."

Reporting in *Road & Track*, John von Neumann said it was "more as though he were airborne than bound to the highway" whilst undertaking some of the high-speed runs. The general consensus of respected competition motorists was that the Porsche was a real driver's machine. With a 0-60 time of 15.4 seconds and a maximum of

Left - The painting and finishing shop in 1953.

The well-finished interior of a 1953 Porsche 356 coupé.

111mph from the 1500 coupé of 1953, the 356 wasn't the fastest sports car available, but it was very competent.

More New Engines

From November 1953, a roller bearing version of the 1300 was made available called the 1300 Super. Launched at the Paris Salon, this 60bhp unit (Type 589) was to be shortlived, only remaining in production for six months; in fact, all pushrod roller-bearing engines would be phased out by the end of 1955.

The most far-reaching engine design of this period came from one of the younger men on the team - Dr. Ernst Fuhrmann. The famous Carrera engine (Type 547) was designed by Fuhrmann with input from Porsche and Rabe. His only brief was to design an engine that

was roughly the same size as the current unit, but capable of producing about twice the power to enable the firm to remain competitive in motorsport. *Carrera*, by the way, is the Spanish word for race, and was subsequently adopted by Porsche following their success on the Carrera Panamerica races.

A Carrera engine was installed in one of the works Gmünd coupes which was entered for the 1954 Liege-Rome-Liege Rally, held that particular year in August. Ferry Porsche's theory was that if the car could last such a tough event, it could safely be put into a production car - Herbert Linge and Helmut Polensky won outright.

The decision to put the engine in a production model was made easy with this fine performance but, to make the unit more suitable for road use, the compression ratio was lowered and the distributors moved to allow better engine access. Now with 100bhp at 6200 rpm and 88lb ft of torque, the 1500GS Carrera was quite a useful motor car. For homologation purposes, 100 were planned.

However, as good as the Carrera engine was in motorsport, its ancestry was starting to show in the road car. Customer complaints were flooding in, but Porsche found an easy solution to the problem - simply telling customers not to run the engine at less than 2500rpm, except for very brief periods. Incidentally, the development of the Carrera engine will be covered in-

depth in the next chapter.

In November 1954, a new crankcase was adopted on the 1.3 and 1.5 litre engines. It was changed from the Volkswagen-style two-piece magnesium alloy to a three-piece aluminium alloy casting, prompting new design numbers. The 1300 was now the Type 506/2, the 1300S was the 589/2, the 1500 Type 546/2 and the 1500S was designated the Type 528/2. In December 1954, the 1100 engine was dropped completely from the range.

The American Market & the Speedster

During 1953, a staff of 437 built 1978 cars. In 1954, the staff increased to 493, but only 1934 cars were produced - 44 less than the previous year. However, on 15 March 1954, the 5000th German-built Porsche was produced (in March 1956 the figure reached 10,000) and exports now accounted for 60 per cent of production.

By 1954, American sales were accounting for a third of Porsche production, and this ratio was still climbing. British vehicles domi-

A smiling Ferry Porsche and workforce with the 5000th German-built Porsche; March 1954.

figure known to be conservative giving a zero-to-60mph time of 13.9 seconds." In fact, in an official timed run, the 1500 Super managed 0-60 in 12.4 seconds.

After all is said and done, the fact remained that the Porsche was just too expensive for Americans in relation to what it offered. Hoffman dealt mainly with Mercedes-Benz, Jaguar, Porsche and Volkswagen; the Volkswagen was an economy car, so in a totally different league. Hoffman suggested that Americans would not spend their money on any sports car with less than 1.5 litres under the bonnet.

John von Neumann, who established Competition Motors in Hollywood in 1948 and was appointed Porsche's West Coast distributor, was the inspiration behind the Speedster. He said "Guys want to go, on a Saturday evening in June, down Sunset Boulevard with their elbow over the door and the girls can see them in the car."

The Speedster was exactly what Hoffman needed to boost sales Stateside, selling at $2995 in basic form. However, for $500 extra, the Speedster could be specified with the 70bhp 1.5 litre engine. This compared very favourably with the $3445 (1500 Coupé) to $4584 (1500S Cabriolet) price range of the other Porsche models.

What Porsche had failed to realise was that when exporting to America, the more basic a vehicle was, the better as far as import taxes were concerned. With a P.O.E

nated the American sports car market at the time, with MG, Triumph and Austin-Healey providing a lot of fun for their customer's money. For the more serious enthusiast, there was always Jaguar and the like.

By 1954, Hoffman was only dealing in 1.5 litre Porsches. Listing most of the extras as cost options, the lower-powered model was

called the "1500 America," while for 1955, he changed this to "1500 Continental." However, objections from Ford (which had the Lincoln Continental) put a halt to this name being used and the America title was resurrected.

Road & Track tested a 1500 Super coupé in September 1954, and noted: "Acceleration of the America is also excellent; a factory

A cabriolet of 1954/5.

The production Speedster. Note the bucket seats and chrome trim along the waistline.

The Speedster was based on the cabriolet, but it was a very different car. This is the prototype, which the author finds quite attractive; others find it ugly.

Below - A seductive promotional shot of the Speedster dating from 1955.

charge calculated on basic car price, the more the car cost, the higher the taxes, which of course had to be passed on to the customer. Optional extras were free of import tax and there was no limit on the number that could be fitted.

Based on the Cabriolet but with minimal equipment, such as a cheap hood, a low and flimsy windscreen and detachable side-screens instead of wind-up windows, the Speedster was introduced into America in September 1954.

The Speedster bodies were also built by Reutter but had lightweight bucket seats and fewer instruments. These, with all the other cost-cutting measures, added up to a weight saving of around 150lbs over the standard convertible, making the Speedster ideal to race in production car events. Engines were 55 or 70bhp 1.5 litre units for the USA, although 1300, 1300S, 1500 and 1500S units were available elsewhere. The Speedster also had a slightly lower axle ratio for better acceleration.

Almost immediately Von Neumann took a Speedster to victory at Torrey Pines, California, and the car quickly gained something of a cult following. Today, one of the most desirable of all 356 models, it is often forgotten that the Speedster was, in fact, an economy model as far as trim and accessories were concerned. It was for this reason that Ferry Porsche was never overly-enthusiastic about the model, as he felt it did the

marque's reputation for high quality more harm than good.

The Press, however, loved it. A 1500S Speedster (or Continental 1500 Speedster) depending on which side of the Atlantic you lived, was tested by *Road & Track* in May

1955. They recorded a 0-60mph time of just 10.3 secs against 12.4 for the coupé. The quarter-mile time was also cut although, due to wind resistance, the top speed of the Speedster was actually less, at 104mph, than the 108mph of the

Right - With the more specialised 550 Spyder on the scene, it was rare to see 356s racing in top class events, although the model was still strongly involved with rallying. However, the Production Class races at the Nürburgring still provided a great deal of entertainment.

that the car was capable of over 125mph, but this seems unlikely.

The 356 engine would find itself in a number of strange applications, ranging from a German-built motorcycle through to industrial, nautical and aerial uses.

More 1954 Motorsport

Engel and Armbrecht won the 1600cc Class of the 1954 Tulip Rally, although the overall winners were Stasse and Gendebien in an Alfa Romeo. Olivier Gendebien would later become associated with the cars from Stuttgart.

The 1954 Mille Miglia saw the International debut of the 550 Spyder and, perhaps, not surprisingly, it won its Class. In the GT Classes, the Hampel/Berghe car won the 1300cc category, while the Von Frankenberg/Sauter machine took the 1600cc title.

The Liège-Rome-Liège Rally was won by the Polensky/Linge pairing in a 1.5 litre 356, confirming the marque's stranglehold on the event. Herbert Linge was born in 1928, and had joined Porsche as an apprentice mechanic in 1949. His name was often seen in the 'fifties in relation to motorsport.

The 1954 Carrera Panamericana was to be the final running of the event. Porsche was again well represented, with four 550 Spyders and two 356s. Becker Estrada and Hirz came sixth and seventh in Class respectively, although even the former's time was some six-and-a-half hours behind

closed car.

In 1955, 1800 Speedsters were built, dropping to 850 in 1956 before rising again in the following year to 1416. In all, a total of 4854 Speedsters were produced, of which only around 25 were right-hand drive (both 356 and 356A type together). The price of a Speedster in America for 1955 was kept at $2995 for the model with the standard engine, but the 1500S went up to $3645.

Perhaps the strangest Porsche special from this period was the twin-engined car produced by Lou Fageol. Fageol had built a mildly-successful twin-engined car for Indianapolis in 1946, but this 1954 Porsche was very strange. With one engine in the front of the Roadster body and the other left in its original position, overall power was supposed to be in the region of 145bhp and with weight more evenly distributed. It has been said

the more specialised 550 of Herrmann.

Art Bunker and Richard Thompson won the SCCA Class F (Production) title in 1954 with a Porsche 1500 Cabriolet. This success was followed up in 1955 when a Speedster won the SCCA Class F title with Bengt Soderstrom at the wheel; even big screen idol James Dean could be seen racing his example, with some success, too, it should be added.

On the 1955 Mille Miglia, Richard von Frankenberg took the 1300cc Special GT Class and R. Günzler collected the 1600cc Gran Turismo trophy. By now, the 550 Spyder was the competition vehicle for Porsche followers to use and it was rare for a 356 to figure in the results when it came to pure racing.

In rallying however, Amman/Suardi won the 1300cc GT Class of the 1955 Tulip Rally, while Andersen and Rottbol-Orum took the 1600cc GT category. Later in the year, in Sweden, the Borgefors/Gustavson pairing won the 1500cc GT Class and overall victory in the

Rally to the Midnight Sun. This was the fourth year in a row that a 1.5 litre Porsche had won the Swedish event outright.

The British Market

The first right-hand drive cars were built in 1951, with the first ever rhd 356 cabriolet going to Australia for the Melbourne Show. At the 1951 Earls Court Show, two Porsche 356 coupes and a cabriolet were put on display by Connaught Cars Ltd. and shown alongside three French Salmsons.

However, Connaught later passed on the Porsche agency to the Volkswagen dealer John Colborne-Baber, as their interest in racing cars took hold. Before long, AFN Ltd. of Isleworth (the people behind Frazer-Nash) came to be the Porsche agents, with imports starting seriously in 1954. That is not to say that before 1954 Porsches were not sold in the UK. Indeed, Colborne Garage of Ripley quoted the following prices for mid-1953 (including tax and duty):

1 litre hardtop - £1971

1 litre convertible - £2200
1.3 litre hardtop - £1842
1.3 litre convertible - £2070
1 litre Super hardtop - £2147
1 litre Super convertible - £2378

These were high prices when one considers an XK120 was around £1600 at this time, and the choice of even cheaper British sports cars was endless. It would explain why only two coupés and a cabriolet were sold in the UK in 1953, all left-hand drive. When the Aldington brothers of AFN became involved, the first car was delivered to them late in 1953 and their first sale (a cabriolet) took place in the January, but they had to wait until May 1954 for the second sale. However, the Press liked the car and judged it on its merits rather than its price.

One of the biggest supporters was Denis Jenkinson. Writing for *MotorSport* in 1955, the year in which he partnered Stirling Moss to a legendary Mille Miglia victory, he said of the Porsche works: "The factory is divided into four departments: machine shop, assembly,

service and racing, the last dealing exclusively with competition motoring, the building of the sports/racing 'Spyder,' the assembly of the four-ohc Carrera engines and experimental work.

"The Porsche is very definitely a handbuilt car, the output being in the order of six or seven cars a day, the assembly line running from the front of the factory to the rear, so that when you arrive in the morning you might see a green coupé joining the line and, by the end of the day, it will be near the end about to receive final adjustments; a continuous flow of about nine or ten cars being on the assembly line. Next door to the Porsche factory is one belonging to Reutter the coachbuilders, and the two are joined by a short private road. This branch of Reutter is occupied solely with Porsche work and, while it is not owned by Porsche, it is under their control as far as work is concerned."

This was a fascinating contemporary insight into the workings of the factory. In 1955, 616 staff built 2952 cars. There was at least one Pre-A Carrera road car built (with a Speedster body) but it would seem, in view of all the evidence, that the Carrera started officially with the 356A models.

It's interesting to note that up until 1955, despite Porsches being such advanced and expensive vehicles, all 356s had no fuel gauge - instead a calibrated wooden dipstick was supplied!

Left - The first right-hand drive cars were built in October 1951. Some were sent to Australia (this picture shows the 1951 Melbourne Show), but Britain was the main target. After a very slow start, the British eventually warmed to the car.

The first design drawing for the Type 356, dated 17 July 1947. Note the similarity to the later 550 Spyder, both in layout and shape.

356 Chassis Numbers

Please note that these are sanction numbers for production runs so they do not necessarily correspond to actual production.

Number One	356-001
Gmünd models	2001 to 2050 and 2052 to 2055
1950 1100	5001 to 5131 and 5163 to 5410
1951 1100	5132 to 5162 and 5411 to 5600 and 10001 to 10170
1951 1300 cabriolet	10350 to 10432
1951 1500 cabriolet	10531 to 11125
1952 1500 cabriolet	10433 to 10469 and 12301 to 12387
1952 1300 coupé	11126 to 12084
1952 1500 coupé	50001 to 50098
1952 1500S	15001 to 15116
1953 1300 coupé	50099 to 51645
1953 1.5 cabriolets	60001 to 60394
1954 1300 coupé	51646 to 53008
1954 1.5 cabriolets	60395 to 60722
1954 1.3 Speedsters	80001 to 80200
1955 1300 coupé	53009 to 55000
1955 1.5 cabriolets	60723 to 61000
1955 1.5 Speedsters	80201 to 81900

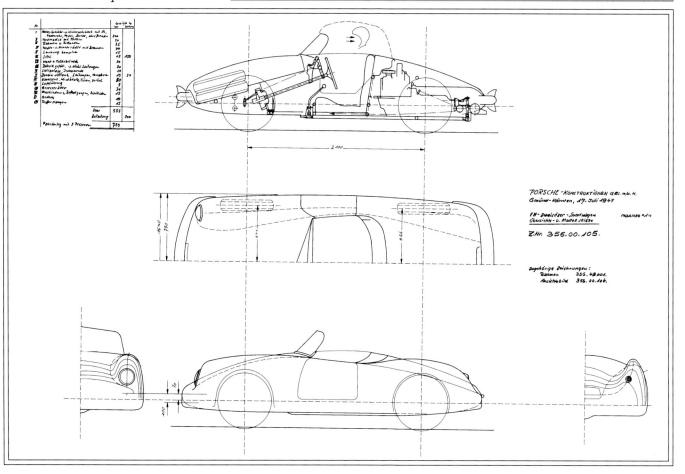

PORSCHE 356

3

550 SPYDER
- ESTABLISHING
A PEDIGREE

The design of the Carrera engine (design 547) has to be credited to Dr. Ernst Fuhrmann, with help from Ferry Porsche and Karl Rabe (Porsche's Chief Engineer). Fuhrmann's brief was to design an engine that was a similar size to the current production unit, but would produce roughly twice the power to enable the company to stay competitive in the world of motorsport.

Design work began in the Summer of 1952. Fuhrmann decided he wanted twin-overhead camshafts on each bank of the flat-four and, in order to keep the physical size of the engine down, devised an ingenious system incorporating no less than nine shafts, fourteen bevel gears and two spur gears. He also designed an efficient dual-entry fan to cool the unit.

The complexity of the new engine made it a difficult unit to develop, but Fuhrmann wanted to see his project finished as quickly as possible. Bruno Trostmann, who was under Fuhrmann at the time, remembers: "For the first six or eight months, he hardly ever let us go home before ten or eleven o'clock at night. He didn't know about holidays."

The 1498cc engine was deliberately designed with oversquare dimensions (bore and stroke of 85 x 66mm) in order to make it a high-revving unit suitable for racing. The crankcase was of aluminium alloy as were the cylinder barrels (bores coated with chrome) and cylinder heads. Twin distributors and coils were employed for the two spark plug per cylinder head design. Roller-bearings were used for the crankshaft and a dry sump engine lubrication system was adopted with an oil cooler (situated at the back of 356 Carreras and in the nose of the Spyder).

There was, of course, a price to pay in terms of power loss through so many moving parts and it could take a specialist mechanic up to 120 hours to build the engine, but the unit's beauty lay in the fact that its overall dimensions were little changed from the standard engine. The first new engine was up and running in April 1953.

Initially 112bhp at 6400rpm was recorded on the testbed (the 547 later proved that it was possible to extract around 180bhp). The new engine was right virtually from the start, although, at first, it had a very narrow power band that came in between 5000 and 7000rpm.

As part of the testing and development regime, the new Carrera engine made its racing debut at the Nürburgring shortly after Le Mans. The event was the sports car race before the German Grand Prix (held 2 August), in which Hans Herrmann and Helm Glockler (Walter Glockler's cousin) were entered by the works in the Le Mans cars (minus hardtops). The third car was the Carrera machine, but it only appeared in practice: Huschke von Hanstein and Hans Herrmann

The Sauter-Porsche pictured in America during 1953 - Stan Mullin owned it at the time.

Below - Ferry Porsche (left) with Walter Glockler.

doing the driving. A week later, the car was loaned to Hans Stuck, the great Grand Prix driver of pre-war days, for the Freiburg-Schauinsland Hillclimb. Hans Herrmann won the event in a rather more standard Porsche, Stuck only managing third. However, despite these early trials, the Carrera engine was not officially announced until the 1954 Mille Miglia for which it was fitted in a 550 Spyder. Herrmann was partnered by Herbert Linge for the event and they took sixth overall - not bad at all for what was officially, if not actually, the Carrera's maiden race.

The Spyder's Predecessors
The Denzel first appeared as a Volkswagen-based special in 1948, but as it was developed over the years, Wolfgang Denzel moved towards Porsche components, particularly their engines. This development produced the winner of the 1300cc Class of the Austrian Alpine Rally in 1954: a fine motor car.

Heinrich Sauter, a Stuttgart businessman, was the originator of another special. The Sauter-Porsche was a lightweight roadster bodied by Hans Klenk and powered by a tuned Porsche 1500 engine. Appearing early in 1951, it failed to finish to Liège-Rome-Liège Rally in August of that year. By the end of 1951, however, Sauter decided the car was not producing the desired results, so he sold it to Francois Picard. Picard duly named it "Le

The fifth Glockler pictured after winning its Class in the Eifelrennen at the Nürburgring. Richard Trenkel accepts the applause, while Huschke von Hanstein can be seen to his left.

Petit Tank" and repainted it in French racing colours; the car was last seen in Europe in the early part of 1952 before it went to America.

Mention must be made of the Mathé Special. Otto Mathé of Innsbruck in Austria had been a Porsche follower from the earliest days (he owned one of the Berlin-Rome cars) and was a remarkable driver considering he had only one arm. He didn't just drive well, he also built a single-seater with Porsche 1500 Super power that performed brilliantly on ice, sand and tarmac. Mathé's car secured a win on its first outing in 1952, beating the legendary Hans Stuck on a Vienna sand track. In the car's final race,

at the 1959 Porsche Memorial Meeting on the frozen lake by Zell-am-See, Mathé (now with 100bhp at his disposal) won against the works Spyder of Richard von Frankenberg!

By far the most successful special, despite the Mathé Special and Denzel's excellent results, was the Glockler. Walter Glockler, Frankfurt's Volkswagen dealer, had raced pre-war and had his garage build him a Volkswagen special to enable him to compete in the German Sports Car Championship. A 58bhp 1.1 litre machine was duly built and it gave Glockler a Class win in 1950. Naturally, as Volkswagen dealers handled the Porsches in those early days, Glockler soon

made use of his contacts. For the 1951 season, a Weidenhausen-bodied "Glockler-Porsche" powered by a 1.5 litre engine made its debut. Sadly, the handling was not a match for the 85bhp engine and 130mph performance and the car was quickly sold on.

The third Glockler model came in time for the 1952 season, this time the car was closely based on the 356. Helm Glockler drove an example to a maiden victory, encouraging his cousin Walter to build more cars. The fourth was campaigned by Hans Stanek and shown on the Porsche stand at both the Geneva and Frankfurt Shows of 1953. The final Glockler (a roadster

Hans Herrmann leading the field at the Nürburgring in August 1953. He went on to win the race, and is seen here being followed by Glockler. Cars from EMW, Borgward and OSCA can also be seen.

Below - The ladder chassis of the 356SL (Type 514) provided the basis for the 550 frame.

Borgwards to take its maiden Class victory (15th overall). This event provided the Porsche company with the foundation stone on which it would build a racing legend.

The 550 Spyder followed the principles laid down by the original Porsche prototype (356.001) almost exactly, having the engine reversed (giving, virtually, a mid-engine layout) to improve handling. It is thought that the tubular ladder frame chassis, designed by Hermann Ramelow, was a modified version of that used on the special 356SL models used at Le Mans. Wheelbase and track dimensions were the same as those of the production road cars.

Erwin Komenda was responsible for the 550's styling and the first five prototypes were built by Weidenhausen (which had built the Glocklers). Usefully, the model's rear-hinged engine cover panel allowed the complete engine, gearbox and ZF limited-slip differential to be lifted out, in one unit, from above.

Chassis 5500001 was the car used at the Nürburgring in May, but in the following month it gained a hardtop similar to that fitted to the second car. These two 550 models were then entered by the works for the 1953 Le Mans 24-Hour Race. Chassis 5500002 was driven by Richard von Frankenberg and Paul Frere (who finished 15th, 1st in Class) and the other car was driven by Hans Herrmann and Helm Glockler (who came home in 16th).

with a 1.1 litre engine) was bought by a Richard Trenkel.

One of the Glocklers was sold to Max Hoffman and raced in the United States with some success. Glockler cars won the 1951 German Hillclimb Championship with Hermann Kathrein (1100 Class) and in 1952 with Hans Breadel (1100 Class). Glockler himself won the 1500 Class in 1951.

It has been said that the Glockler-Porsches were the impetus behind the works deciding to build its own Spyder (Type 550) and there is a similarity of design between the cars.

Glockler would continue to be linked with the Porsche marque for a number of years to come.

Birth of the Spyder

The 550 Spyder made its debut on 31 May 1953 for the Eifelrennen at the Nürburgring. On this occasion, the car was powered by a 1500 Super engine and, driven by Helm Glockler, it narrowly beat the

54

Left - Rear view of one of the cars prepared for the 1954 Le Mans 24-hour Race. The hardtops were added to the Spyder bodies as the regulation screen height dictated that a closed coupé would be the most aerodynamic.

Bottom left - This picture of 5500004 clearly shows the Carrera engine. The binnacle in front of the driver housed the central rev-counter, with the tachometer to the left and oil temperature and fuel level gauges on the right. This car was later rebodied for racing.

Below - Chassis 5500004 (the "Humpback") with some young VIPs - Ferry Porsche's sons. Wolfgang is seen standing by the car, while behind (from the left) are Peter, Gerd and Butzi. Butzi would go on to style the 904 racer and the 911 road car.

Neither car had the Carrera engine at this stage, so only 78bhp was available which allowed a top speed of around 125mph.

Chassis 5500003 was the car tested with the Carrera engine at the Nürburgring in August. Strangely, the same car was entered in 1953 Liège-Rome-Liège Rally with a 1500 Super engine installed. It crashed out of the latter event anyway, so a Carrera engine wouldn't have helped its cause.

Chassis 5500004 was the "Humpback" car shown at the 1954 Brussels Show. It was the only one of this design built, but it did have the Carrera engine. It also featured knock-off wheels, but it was found that the 550 was so light that tyre wear was minimal and frequent changes unnecessary.

The fifth car was shown at the 1953 Paris Salon and was almost the same as the 'production' models.

By the early part of 1954, the first of the customer cars were being completed by Wendler of Reutlingen. The 1500 Super engine was used, but tuning and a 12:1 compression ratio brought the power up to around 100bhp. The official designation of this model was 550/1500RS: the 1500 standing for the engine capacity, and RS for *Rennsport*. However, Max Hoffman coined the name "Spyder" and it was this title that stuck in the public mind. Two were sold in 1954, sixty three in the following year, and thirteen in 1956.

The 1953 Carrera Panamericana

The "Carrera Panamericana" race was instigated in 1950 to celebrate the opening of the Pan-American highway, planned to run from Alaska to Tierra del Fuego in Mexico.

Although it did not receive much attention in Britain (even when it became a round of the World Sportscar Championship), it was very well publicised in America.

Porsche's link with Mexico came about through an exhibition in Stuttgart during the Summer of 1952. Count Berckheim had just returned from the Mille Miglia and managed to obtain the Porsche distribution rights for Mexico for his cousin, Prince Alfonso von Hohenlohe, already a distributor

Left - A Wendler-bodied customer car - the production models were roughly 85lb heavier than the works machines. Note the Spyder badge on the front wing and the final rear light/wing arrangement.

Bottom left - Chassis 5500005 as a Show Car. It was later prepared for racing, losing its knock-off wheels.

Below - The works' cars for the 1953 Carrera Panamerica at the Von Hohenlohe garage. Sadly, both cars failed to finish.

for Volkswagen in Mexico City. The cars used on the 1952 Carrera were the first two Porsches to arrive there (see Chapter Two). For 1953, there would be a true works' effort.

Sponsored by Fletcher Aviation of Pasadena, Texas (this company was considering building small helicopters powered by Porsche engines and had already built a multi-purpose Porsche-powered

Jose Herrarte Ariano proudly poses next to the ex-works' 550 that he took to First in Class in the 1953 Carrera Panamericana. The hardtop from Le Mans had been left on.

Jeep), Wendell Fletcher's only request was that the two works' cars appear in a race in America before their main event - unfortunately both works' cars retired in Georgia after a good start. This was the first appearance for the Porsche works' team on the American continent.

Huschke von Hanstein pictured in 1954 with a customer 550 Spyder.

The Competition Shop at Porsche, with the cars being prepared for the ill-fated 1955 Le Mans 24-hour Race. Ferry Porsche is seen on the left talking to journalists.

The Porsche contingent of Huschke von Hanstein, Hans Herrmann, Karl Kling, Herbert Linge, Werner Enz and Willi Enz then travelled to Mexico for the start. Held from 19 to 23 November, the 1600cc Sport Class of the 1953 Carrera Panamericana was totally dominated by the Porsche marque.

The works' drivers were Hans Herrmann (chassis 5500005) and Karl Kling (5500004). Herrmann was born in 1928 and started his racing career in Porsche GTs in 1951 but, despite this late start, he was very quick and later became the German Sports Car Champion in a Porsche Spyder. Kling was another proven winner, having been with Mercedes-Benz in 1952, when he won a number of events including the Carrera.

Sadly both works' cars were out by the second leg of the Panamerica, Herrmann through mechanical problems and Kling through an accident (at one point everyone thought Kling had been killed, but thankfully he arrived safely in Puebla).

Fortunately for Porsche, two Le Mans coupes had been bought and entered by the Guatemalan garage owner, Jaroslav Juhan. The winner of the 1600cc Class (and 32nd overall) was Jose Herrarte Ariano in 5500002; Juhan had retired 5500001 when its distributor drive failed. The Panamerica could have ended in disaster but for the privateers - in the end, the Porsches won five out of the eight stages. Fernando Segura's 356 Super came second in Class and 33rd overall.

It was a hard first year for the Spyder but, with the new Carrera engine, it would become easier in the future.

Competition in 1954

The 1954 Mille Miglia, which started on the 1 May, was the international debut of the 550 Spyder with the new Carrera engine. The top finisher for Porsche was the 550 Spyder driven by Hans Herrmann and Herbert Linge. After having had a close call with a train on a level

A 550 Spyder with aerodynamic aids at Solitude. The Solitude circuit was a normal road to the southwest of Stuttgart which was sealed off for racing once a year.

crossing (they ducked underneath the barriers in the low car, only seconds before the train thundered through), they went on to finish sixth overall and first in the 1500cc Sports Class. Porsche also did well in the GT Classes.

In the next month, at Le Mans, three 550 Spyders with Carrera engines were entered by the works. The car driven by Johnny Claes and Paul Stasse came 12th overall and, following an accident involving the leading OSCAs, won its Class. The Richard von Frankenberg/Helm Glockler machine retired in the first hour. The Hans Herrmann/Helmut Polensky car also retired.

The works also entered a fourth Spyder. Driven by the Gonzague Olivier/Zora Arkus-Duntov (the Chief Development Engineer at Chevrolet) pairing, this car was fitted with a 1.1 litre engine and came 14th overall (first in Class). It's interesting to note that the smaller machine was only 100 miles down on the 1.5 litre 550 at the end of the 24 hours. The similar-looking Porsches at Le Mans were identified by different colours on the rear wing tops (red, blue, green and yellow were used).

Hans Herrmann led the Porsches home in a one, two, three, four victory in the sports car race before the European Grand Prix at the Nürburgring. In the Tour de France Automobile, Claude Storez and Herbert Linge won the Sports Class in a Spyder and, closer to home, Richard von Frankenberg did likewise in the AVUS races, with Polensky winning the GT category.

What was, sadly, to be the last Carrera Panamericana started from Tuxtla Gutierrez on the 19 November 1954. The smaller-engined category for sports cars was divided at 1500cc instead of the previous year's 1600cc, but the Porsches were still safe for the time being.

After a slow start, which saw the Borgward team take the first two stages and the OSCA of Louis Chiron the third, the Porsches came back to win the remaining five. The Sport Class was won by Hans Herrmann, with Jaroslav Juhan second. Chiron's OSCA came third, with the 550 of Segura fourth. The 550 of Salvador Lopez Chavez and 356s of Becker Estrada and Hirz took the next three places in that order.

What was, perhaps, of even greater significance was that Herrmann had managed to achieve third place overall (less than two hours down on Maglioli's winning Ferrari), while Juhan took fourth overall, just seconds behind his team mate. Segura was 12th overall, with the other Porsches coming in 28th, 67th and 70th respectively.

Claude Storez and Herbert Linge's 550 in the 1954 Tour de France Automobile.

Richard von Frankenberg giving Helmut Polensky (with camera) a lift. Both won their races at the famous AVUS track on 19 September 1954.

Competition in 1955

1955 was quite a lean year for the Spyder. Guatemalan-based Jaroslav Juhan had some fine results with his 550 racer, especially in the Buenos Aires 1000km, where he won his class as

Hans Herrmann in the 550 Spyder that he took to third overall on the 1954 Carrera Panamerica.

Below right - A 550 Spyder on the AVUS banking during the 1955 Avusrennen. Held at the end of September, Richard von Frankenberg won the event from a pair of EMWs.

Porsche poster making the most of 1955 Tourist Trophy successes.

he had in 1954. Class wins followed at Sebring in March in the 12-hour Race and, two months later, in the Mille Miglia, there was eighth overall and a 1500cc Sports Class win for Wolfgang Seidel. The Rhine Cup Race at Hockenheim was a Porsche one-two-three (Von Frankenberg winning).

At Le Mans in June, a fine performance from Porsche was overshadowed by the tragic loss of many lives. The Von Frankenberg/Polensky 550 Spyder not only won its 1500cc Class and the Index of Performance, but also came fourth overall (around 200 miles down on the winning Jaguar D-type).

A 550, entered by Ecurie Belge, came fifth, driven by Olivier Gendebien (his first Le Mans) and Wolfgang Seidel. Helm Glockler and Jaroslav Juhan drove a works' car to sixth place overall and two other 550s finished - 13th (first in the 1100cc Class) and 18th. Only one Porsche, a private entry, failed to finish.

An impressive line of Porsches about to enter the arena at Le Mans 1955.

An interesting picture showing the 550 Spyder being flown out to Caracus for the race held there on 6 November. Von Hanstein took eighth place, with Fangio (Maserati) winning at an average speed of 82mph.

550 Spyder Chassis Numbers

There is only one batch of 550 chassis numbers; the first five cars were classed as prototypes, although they were kept within the same sequence as the works racers and customer cars.

550/RS1500 Spyder   5500001 to 5500090

The Porsche five-speed gearbox made its debut in the 1955 Tourist Trophy, which began on 2 September. Carroll Shelby and Masten Gregory ran away with the 1500cc Class, followed home by two more Porsches. This all-American team did a lot for the 550 Spyder in the States, but at $6500 a time, it remained a car for the serious racer only.

The 550 had proved itself better on long fast circuits, where its reliability and sheer speed showed through. On the tighter tracks, the lighter and better handling Lotus and Cooper machines were definitely ahead, but Porsche had something up its corporate sleeve - the 550A with a lighter and stronger spaceframe chassis.

Porsche had not forgotten its roots, however, despite all this racing activity. Denis Jenkinson, writing in *MotorSport* in 1955, said: "Competition is a byword at the Porsche factory and the Porsche car is a perfect example of a race-bred one, the 1956 models all being available with the Carrera engine."

It's ironic, in view of its racing successes, that the death of movie star James Dean at the wheel of his 550 Spyder gave the model its greatest public fame. Supplied with the Spyder by John von Neumann from new, Dean was on his way to a race in Salinas, in September 1955, when he collided head on with an oncoming vehicle.

4

THE 356A

Introduced at the Frankfurt Show in September 1955, the 356A had the modified T-1 (*Technische Programm 1*) body. The car's length was the same as the previous model at a fraction over 155 inches, the width was the same at 65.5 inches, as was the wheelbase at 82.5 inches, but there were subtle changes.

It may seem trivial, but the curved windscreen was perhaps the new model's best distinguishing point. The technology simply wasn't available to make curved windscreens economically when the first Porsche appeared, and later, when Porsche introduced its one-piece glass screen, the distinctive original vee was left in the design. The 356A's screen was smooth, and the roofline adjusted to suit. Incidentally, the windscreen was designed to pop out in a head-on crash.

Rubbing strips were added below the doors (like those on the Speedster) and the spare wheel was repositioned to give extra luggage space. For the 356A, Porsche became the first manufacturer to fit a windscreen washer as standard, deeming such a device necessary because the car's aerodynamic nose

A 1956 Carrera GS coupé. Note the Carrera badges on the front wing and tail and also the rubbing strip along the sill added to all 356A models.

The simple but functional dashboard of the Speedster. This model had a different interior to the coupé and cabriolet.

directed road dirt straight onto the screen. The dashboard was changed slightly and reclining seats, by Reutter of Stuttgart, became a feature. However, the main changes were under the skin. The floor was lowered to make access easier and there was better sound-proofing, too.

Different suspension rates, a new anti-roll bar and better shock absorbers (now mounted vertically instead of at an angle) combined with wider, smaller diameter road wheels fitted with crossply tyres all added up to handling that was far more neutral than before.

When the 1100 Class was dropped, the powers that be moved the old 1500 Class break to 1600 for international competition. In response, Porsche introduced the 1582cc engine (the increase being obtained through larger bores) in 1955. There were two versions available, the 1600 (Type 616/1) and 1600 Super (Type 616/2) giving 60 or 75bhp respectively. The 1300 (Type 506/2) and 1300 Super (Type 589/2) continued unchanged for the time being in most markets, but the 1300 models had been dropped in America during the Spring of 1955.

The 1500GS Carrera engine was displayed alongside the new 356A range at the 1955 Frankfurt Show and, like the other power-units, was available in the updated Coupé, Cabriolet or Speedster bodyshells. Although the open cars were nowhere near as aerodynamic

as the coupé, the brute force of the Carrera engine made up for it - the Carrera engine option, with 100bhp on tap, made for a very quick motor car. However, its designer, Ernst Fuhrmann, left Porsche in 1956.

Options on the new models included the usual radio and spotlight choices, but there was also an auxiliary heater offered. Seven standard colour schemes were listed (each with various interior options) and there were four special paint colours available at extra cost.

On the 1 December 1955, the old Porsche Stuttgart works was, at last, handed back to its rightful owner. Called *Werk I* by Porsche, the original works was quickly occupied by management, along with the design, experimental and racing departments and the repair shop.

Towards the end of 1955, three out of every four cars produced by Porsche (which by now employed around 600 people) were exported, the majority of which found their way to America.

The New Car in America

The first public showing of the 356A

in the United States was at New York Show in April 1956. By now, American specification vehicles had gained bumper over-riders and these were adopted across the range (for all markets) after July 1956.

Many of the changes to the 356A were brought about in response to the growing sales in America - the world's largest market for sports cars. To make the cars more user-friendly for novice drivers the anti-roll bar was thickened and the steering and suspension geometry were changed to make the car feel more stable going into corners.

Max Hoffman had used the "Continental" name for a short time in 1955 for the Porsche 1500 models, but Ford were already using this name in their Lincoln range so, when Ford protested, the name was promptly discontinued by Hoffman to avoid a law suit. Therefore, when the 356A came along, the 1500 was the "America" although a number of cars carried a "European" badge. By the end of the 356A run, Hoffman had scrapped the naming of models and instead used the official Porsche designations.

For 1956, prices in America

The "European" badge, as used briefly in America.

A delightful period picture of the 356A Speedster. The Carrera model had a "Carrera" badge underneath the "Speedster" script on the front wing, and under the "Porsche" badge at the back. The Speedster chrome trim along the waistline was later added to a number of models.

varied enormously. The Speedster was $3215 with the standard 1600 engine, while the 1600 Super cost around $400 more. The 1600 coupé and cabriolet were priced at $3665 and $3915 respectively, and again, the Super power-unit added around $400. However, the Carrera engine added $2000 to the base prices so, at $5915, the drophead Carrera model was only $500 short of the price of a Cadillac Eldorado. Put another way, at $3150 each, the American buyer could have very nearly bought two Ford Thunderbirds for the same price!

Typical options for the Speedster were coupé-style seats at $45 or detachable side windows at $10 a pair. Rudge knock-off centre-lock wheels were available throughout the late 'fifties at about $600 a set, but they were not allowed in Germany.

One of the Porsches on the Liège-Rome-Liège rally, this one driven by Smissen and Ruberecht.

Although American distribution was by now being handled by the Porsche of America Corporation of Teaneck, New Jersey, Hoffman was still directly involved with importation of Porsches into America until 1964.

Competition in 1956

The Monte Carlo Rally of 1956 was to be Ronnie Adams' because he brought his Mk.VII Jaguar home ahead of a mixed bag of competitors. Porsche honour was upheld by privateers: the Coupé de la Condamine was awarded to the 1.3 litre 356 of A. Gacon and H. Arcan. The coveted Coupé des Dames went to M. Blanchoud and L. Alziary who, like Gacon, started from Lisbon. It's interesting to note that a Volkswagen Beetle finished fifth overall, driven by W. Levy and K. Kotott. If nothing else, it was a Porsche design!

Gacon and Arcan took overall victory in the Lyon-Charbonnieres Rally (it was actually a Porsche one, two) and there were Class wins for Porsche in both the Geneva Rally and the Tulip Rally. Jean Behra took a very respectable fifth place on the Tour de France Automobile and no less than three Porsche drivers won a Coupé des Alpes in 1956: P. Strahle, R. Buchet and W. Rickert.

On the racing front, the Mille Miglia saw the debut of the 550A Spyder (similar to the 550 but with a spaceframe chassis). However, it was a poor showing by Porsche's previous standards in the event, with just the Persson/Blomquist 356 taking a Class win in the 1600cc Touring/GT category.

After the success in the face of adversity of the previous year, the 1956 Le Mans 24-hour Race was something of a disappointment. Apart from the Richard von Frankenberg/Wolfgang von Trips car, which took fifth overall, the Stuttgart concern had only one other finisher out of six entries. This was a 1.3 litre 356A Coupé entered and driven by Bourel but, although placed 13th, the reality was that it came in last but one. The works Carrera 1500 of Nathan and Glockler retired less than halfway through.

The only works Carrera coupé in the 1956 Le Mans event, it retired after nine hours.

Production Changes

The first Porsche police cars were supplied in 1956 to the German *Polizei*. Later cars were sent to police forces in Holland, Switzerland, Sweden, Finland and Japan - in fact, the very last 356s ever built went to the Dutch police.

The 10,000th German-built car was completed on 16 March 1956 (a metallic blue coupé). Although there was an improvement in the gearbox casing in 1956, generally there were less changes to the cars as production rose. When Porsche was a small scale operation, it had been easy to make frequent changes as parts were ordered in smaller numbers. Now, economics dictated buying in large quantities and thus things stayed the same for longer.

At the end of 1956, William Boddy of *MotorSport* went to the Porsche works. He had this to say: "The rear-engined, air-cooled flat-four Porsche is now well and truly established as a compact, beautifully-proportioned high-performance car - in fact, there is no other car quite like it.

"Coming from a country where, although considerable enthusiasm exists for limited production, handbuilt sports cars, the firms that produce them are very small indeed, it was heartening to find the demand so great that 700-750 workers are employed in building 20 Porsches a day. They work under conditions normally associated only with a racing car factory, the benches and floor in the one big

assembly hall spotlessly clean and skilled labour employed for the more complicated of the assembly processes.

"The layout of the Porsche assembly line is simplicity itself. In the well-lit assembly hall the bodyshells arrive on trolleys from the adjacent Reutter coachwork factory. They then proceed along a U-shaped assembly line, the suspension components and detail fittings being attached as the cars move along the first leg of the U, the power-units and components being added as they progress along the remaining leg, until complete cars, ready for road-test, emerge side-by-side with the body shells entering the factory. Each stage of assembly occupies 22 minutes, as

Ferry Porsche with the 10,000th German-built car. The tradition of celebrating the milestones in production continues to this day.

Below - A 356A with Glockler wire wheels, seen here at a concours competition in Bad Homburg. German regulations are very strict on what can and can't be fitted to vehicles, so Glockler must have had a series of products approved by the TUV.

skilled fitters and mechanics go about their tasks, after which the car is moved on to the next operation towards completion.

"Beside the assembly line is the assembly bay, the engine crankcase being held in a rotatable jig running on a waist-high rail, so that as each step in engine assembly is completed the jig can be rolled over to the next fitter on the line, the entire unit being turned over as required. Six or seven fitters build up each engine. Castings are supplied by a local foundry but women are set to work on them with electrically-driven wire brushes, polishing ports and smoothing the insides of the manifolds before assembly. Pistons are warmed on electric stoves to ensure the correct relationship of expansion between piston and rings before they are inserted in the cylinder barrels.

"When each engine is completed it is taken on a trolley to a test-house outside the assembly hall and run on one of a pair of Schenck-Waage water dynamometers for a period of four hours. In this test-house, there is no evidence of noise, heat or fumes, but here every engine - note, every engine - is thoroughly tested, an hour's running being done at 3000 rpm followed by half-an-hour idling, then 1 hour at 5000 rpm, followed by a final half-hour of fluctuating throttle openings. A book is kept in the engine test-house in which full details of each test are entered,

atmospheric pressure and air temperature at the time being first recorded. At the end of the test period a horsepower check is taken and any engine which does not come very close to normal is stripped down for examination by a staff separate from the fitters who assembled the engine. This is not the end of Porsche testing, because every car is driven on the road for one hour.

"It is taken as a matter of course that wheel balancing, a micrometer check of tolerances in roller-bearings for the gearbox, etc., and a final test that the front wheels are correctly aligned, are undertaken.

"The staff works from 7am to 5.30pm five days a week, and the racing staff all hours of the day and night as required. Incidentally, tools have to be drawn from the stores, signed for each morning and handed in at night and the spotlessly clean spanners, etc., are laid out on the benches like surgical instruments.

"We had only been in the factory for a matter of minutes before our eyes alighted on a battery of 16 steering boxes being motored electrically, from full lock to full lock, a process which goes on for some three hours (equal to 3500 miles of driving) to ensure a perfectly smooth steering action when the customer drives away in his car."

William Boddy's account gave a fascinating contemporary insight into the workings of the factory and provided the reader with information on a number of changes employed during 356 production from its earlier years. Walter Schmidt was named as the head of Sales, and Klaus von Rücker (ex-Studebaker) was in charge of the Technical & Experimental Department.

Autosport, in their report of 31 August 1956, said: "The whole process of building cars is done under surgical conditions of cleanliness, and each man has his tools laid out on a felt pad in a predetermined order; there are no loose spanners on the bench or on the floor." Getting on to the serious business of testing cars, *Autosport's* reporter went on: "As a competition car, the Carrera is obviously the job, but for road work I prefer the Super. The latter is, in fact, the quicker of the two from a standstill to 60mph, taking about a level 10 seconds compared with the 10.4 or so of the 'racer.' Of course, the Carrera has

more 'steam' once the revs rise, and has 10mph more maximum speed. Nevertheless, it requires almost constant use of the gearlever, while the bigger engine is surprisingly flexible."

The tester noted that the 1956 cars felt livelier than the previous year's models, but it was in the areas of suspension and roadholding that the new Porsche showed the greatest improvement. "That tail-heavy feeling has gone, and the average driver would not be conscious that this is a rear-engine car. The suspension feels harder than before, and a much steadier ride is given at speeds over 100mph. The car also handles better in fast bends."

More Changes
Teardrop tail lights replaced the twin round items in March 1957 and the front indicators gained a larger chrome surround at the same time. In addition, the rear window on the Speedster and Cabriolet models was made slightly larger. The improved Type 644 transmission was gradually phased-in during the year, but by far the biggest changes came when the T-2 body was introduced at the 1957 Frankfurt Show.

The 1300 models were dropped from the range and the 1600 Super engine now had plain bearings, but retained aluminium/chrome-coated cylinders; the strict 1600 now featured cheaper but quieter cast-iron cylinders and new Zenith

The 1958 model year cabriolet. Note the exhaust exits in the over-riders (showing this to be a 1.6 litre model), the new rear lights and larger back window.

carburettors were employed improving low-speed performance. Although these changes were quite significant, the power outputs remained the same, as did the engine Type numbers.

The twin exhausts of the 1600 models now ran through the rear over-riders and although this has been dismissed by some as nothing more than a gimmick to please the Americans, it was actually to increase ground clearance. A diaphragm clutch was fitted, which was lighter to use, and the steering was improved. The cam-and-roller steering came from the ZF company and was fitted with a damper.

Bodily, the B-post was modified slightly and the floor strengthened for the provision of seatbelts. For comfort during the winter months, a fibreglass hardtop was made available for the open cars. To make this possible on the cabriolet, the hood was made removable and the area around where it sat modified to allow the fitting of a mounting kit. Also in 1957, the side windows gained quarterlights on the cabriolet and they were offered as an option on the closed car.

The Carrera Models

On the final Mille Miglia, which began 12 May, the 356 of Strahle/Linge came away with a Class win in the GT category. Following the Frankfurt Show in 1957, the Carrera became available in two versions - a De Luxe (GS) model with different carburation and an improved heater, and the GT. The GT was available only as a Speedster or coupé and was aimed squarely at competition.

Denis Jenkinson wrote in *MotorSport* magazine: "In the meantime, Porsche racing, development and production were continuing to work hand-in-hand and the 1500GS engine was in full-scale production, this being the flat-four 1 litre unit for four shaft-driven overhead camshafts, identical apart from the compression ratio

to the engines used in Spyders and RS models. Other racing items transferred to the production cars were steering gear, brakes, carburettors, shock absorbers, front suspension geometry advances and ignition arrangements.

"The interesting thought is - when will the low-pivot rear axle be available in production, for all good things on the works cars come to the public in the end. It was not many years ago that Porsche won the Liege-Rome-Liege with a special car having a four-camshaft engine; now you can buy that engine over the counter. Before that the early Porsches had crash-type gearboxes and at one race a factory car appeared with a synchromesh box and now all Porsches have the all-synchromesh box, and so it goes on - design, racing, development

and production ..."

There was 110bhp on tap, a larger fuel tank, bigger front brakes (from the Spyder) and weight was saved wherever possible, even down to complete removal of the heater and hub caps and the use of lighter bumpers minus the over-riders. The 1500GT Speedster was available in America at $5305 (or £2926 in Britain) against $5215 for the GS. By the following year, the GT was moved further towards pure competition work with a lightweight alloy engine cover, doors and front hood.

Carrera GS road car engines took less time to build because the GT had hand-finished ports, radiused manifold curves, different cams to give the larger valves more lift and a higher compression ratio. Helmut Bott said of the Car-

Right - The Speedster that took World Records at Monza in March 1957. Note the aero screen, the full tonneau cover, and fairing behind the driver's head to aid aerodynamics.

Below - A 1500GS Carrera cabriolet with optional hardtop.

Bottom - Porsches awaiting collection at Stuttgart Airport in September 1957.

rera: "At first we expected to build only a very small series, but demand was far higher than we thought, and the Carrera had a good name despite some service problems." However, this popularity led to production difficulties. Therefore, the Type 692 engine was

74

introduced. For this engine the crankshaft roller-bearings were replaced by a plain bearings and, although the Carrera was a little late catching up with the FIA regulations, the engine's capacity was increased to 1587cc by enlarging the bore to 87.5mm. Power output was 115bhp at 6200rpm and there was 100lb ft of torque.

Klaus von Rücker was the man behind the change to plain crankshaft bearings for the Carrera - roller-bearings were simply too much hassle for anything but very limited production. Having said that, a number of Carreras were built up with roller-bearings after the change point.

The 1600GS engine could be specified with all body options (a coupé was £3061 in the UK, with test results showing a top speed of 115mph and a 0-60 time of 12.0

Right - The Convertible D of 1958. This must be a very early car as the wing badge says "Speedster D" - the name was changed before production commenced.

Paul Strahle and Herbert Linge on their way to a Class victory on the last Mille Miglia.

seconds), while the 1600GT was available only as a coupé or, for a short while at least, as a Speedster. The road/race car link was more obvious in the Carrera, with real life situations and experiences on the track benefiting the road car buyer - a 1.6 litre Carrera had first been tested on the Freiburg hillclimb in 1957.

Death of the Speedster

In March 1957, Rolf Goetze's Carrera Speedster (fitted with a special 1529cc engine, full tonneau and aero-screen) had created new two litre World Records for 1000 miles, 2000km and 12-hours, with one lap of the Monza track being covered at an impressive 128.4mph - about the race average during the Italian Grand Prix of that year.

At Le Mans, the French-entered 1.5 litre 356A Speedster driven by Slotine and Bourel retired: piston trouble in the fourth hour sidelined the car. The vast majority of the Porsche entry that year retired before race end.

There were Class wins on the 1957 Tulip Rally and the German Rally as well. A Carrera Speedster won the 1957 Liège-Rome-Liège Rally (Marathon de la Route) in the hands of Claude Storez and he also took Index of Performance honours and fifth overall in the Tour de France Automobile of the same year.

In July 1958, the American magazine *Motor Trend* carried out a test on the 1600 Super Speedster and noted: "Contrary to the opinion that sports cars must have stiffer springing, Porsche has proven that roadability is improved through softer springing. This theory, combined with the 88hp 1600 engine and the suspension components taken from the Spyders, has produced new improved handling characteristics."

Sports Car Illustrated clocked the Carrera Speedster at 125.5mph and a British magazine managed exactly the same. Through the gears, first gave 37mph, second 70mph and third gear 90mph. The 0-60mph yardstick was covered in just 10.8 seconds. *Speed Age* said: "Probably not since the days of the Bugatti has any sports car exerted upon its owner the dynamic kind of fascination peculiar to the Porsche."

The thing was, the Speedster simply wasn't selling in big enough numbers. Best estimates, for that is all they are, show that 148 Carrera Speedsters were built: 71 of them GT versions aimed at competition work (at such a high price it is hardly surprising so few were built).

The American magazine, *Car and Driver*, summed up the Speedster in one statement: "What counted with the Speedster was that it was an ugly little bathtub of a car that was dirt simple, bordered on the unbreakable and went like stink." The standard-engined

A selection of 356As await despatch outside Werk II *in 1958. Note the new wheel trims with the Porsche badge in the centre.*

Below - Porsche Speedsters racing at Laguna Seca in June 1958. The Porsche continued to be as popular as ever in American racing, and just as successful too. Dickey (number 20) took a Class win on this occasion.

Speedsters gave the Stuttgart firm very little in the way of profit, especially with a fluctuating dollar, so they were simply not viable unless they sold in high volume. Unfortunately, not enough people were willing to sacrifice comfort for the sake of the Speedster's marginally better performance.

In August 1958, the Speedster was superseded by the Speedster D (the D being added in recognition of the coachbuilders, Drauz of Heilbronn) with a more serviceable hood, a better windscreen, padded seats and wind-up side windows - it was much more in line with Ferry Porsche's ideals. However, before sales to the public began, the name was changed to Convertible D in order to distance it from the old Speedster.

Making its debut at the Paris Show, the Convertible D was more luxurious and gave the Stuttgart firm a far higher profit margin. Drauz was used because Reutter were already operating at their maximum capacity. However, a little-known fact is that twenty-five 1600GT Carrera Speedsters were built in 1959 and sold to selected customers purely for racing.

Other 1959 News

"The four-speed all-synchro transmission works like a hot knife through butter, fully justifying its use by Ferrari and Maserati in their racing juggernauts" said one magazine. August 1958 saw another magazine describing "the finest and

fastest synchromesh transmission in the world." In December 1958 the Type 716 transmission was introduced; it was even easier to use, due to a further improvement of the Porsche synchromesh, but less delicate to handle.

Class wins continued to be awarded to Porsche drivers throughout the 1958 rally season.

The Storez/Buchet pairing took their category in the Lyon-Charbonnieres Rally and the Porsche of Schorr and Poll took its Class in the Tulip Rally. Later in the year, Walter and Strahle teamed up for a Class win on the German Rally.

Incidentally, in the early part of 1958, Claude Storez, the French

Ferry Porsche, pictured in 1958, with the empire he created. How times had changed in just one decade!

GT Champion, had Zagato build an attractive lightweight open body on his Carrera GT chassis. After completion, it was driven to the Porsche works for tuning but, unfortunately, was destroyed in an accident shortly after leaving Zuffenhausen. Sadly, shortly afterwards, Claude Storez died in a crash.

On the racing front, the most noteworthy results came in the Sebring 12-hour Race when

Huschke von Hanstein and Herbert Linge took their Class. Sepp Gregor took an overall victory on the Rossfeld hillclimb.

In 1959, Gorris and Wiedouw took their Class in the Tulip Rally and a Porsche once again took its Class in the German Rally. The 1959 Liège-Rome-Liège Rally (or Marathon de la Route) was won outright by Strahle and Buchet in a 1.6 litre Carrera, despite gearbox problems towards the end. Paul

Ernst Strahle was, by the way, the Volkswagen and Porsche dealer for Schorndorf.

A Carrera Speedster won its Class in the Targa Florio (with a 130bhp engine and special gear ratios). A little while after, at the Nürburgring 1000km Race, disc brakes were tried by Porsche for the first time; they were fitted to the 356A of Walter and Strahle who managed a Class win. It was noted that the Carrera GT coupés of 1959

Strahle and Buchet on their way to victory on the 1959 Liège-Rome-Liège rally. It was an incredibly hard event that year, with only 14 finishers from a field of 97.

were lapping the Nürburgring as quickly as the early 550 Spyders when they were first introduced.

Aero-engines

Aero-engines have been associated with Professor Porsche from his earliest days in engineering; indeed the first such project he was involved with can be traced back to 1908. The reader would be excused for wondering what on earth that has to do with this book but, at the 1959 German Industrial Fair, Porsche exhibited a range of new aero-engines based on the same unit used in the 356A.

The 1582cc engines used a 12v electrical system, dry sump lubrication and twin-plugs per cylinder, but were otherwise remarkably like those used for the Porsche road cars. After four years of testing, the Company launched four aircraft power-units - the Type 678/1 (65bhp), 678/3 (52bhp), 678/3A (52bhp but with electric starter) and 678/4 (75bhp). The 678/1 used a single downdraught carburettor, while the other three engines had twin-carburettors.

Prices ranged from 4115DM to 5860DM. It should also be noted that in 1961, the Gyrodyne one-man helicopter appeared: it was powered by a Type 702 Porsche engine, a development of the 678/3.

LE MARATHON DE LA ROUTE 1959

356A Chassis Numbers

Approximately 559 356A models were built in 1955. A total 4201 cars were built in 1956 and 5241 (3705 of which had the T-1 body) in 1957. The total for 1958 was 5994 vehicles and during 1959, the final year of the 356A, no less than 4656 cars were produced before the new model made its debut at that year's Frankfurt Show.

1955 coupé	55001 to 55390
1955 cabriolet	61001 to 61069
1955 Speedster	81901 to 82000
1956 coupé	55391 to 58311
1956 cabriolet	61070 to 61499
1956 Speedster	82001 to 82189
1957 1.3 coupé	58312 to 59090
1957 1.3 cabriolet	61500 to 61700
1957 1.3 Speedster	82190 to 83691
1957 1.6 coupé	100001 to 102504
1957 1.6 cabriolet	61701 to 61892
	and 150001 to 150149
1957 1.6 Speedster	83792 to 84366
Carrera coupé	12235 to 12387
1958 1.6 coupé	102505 to 106174
1958 1.6 cabriolet	150150 to 151531
1958 1.6 Speedster	84367 to 84922
1958 Convertible D	85501 to 85886
1959 1.6 coupé	106175 to 108917
1959 1.6 cabriolet	151532 to 152475
1959 Convertible D	85887 to 86830

A 1950 Model Year Gmünd coupé (the wheels are from a later 356). It is very rare indeed to see a Gmünd-built Porsche nowadays.

Ferdinand Anton Ernst Porsche photographed in 1994 on his 85th birthday with Porsche Number One and a 911 Carrera. Ferry Porsche has been an excellent ambassador for Germany and the motor industry in general.

The 356 coupé of 1954. A choice of nine body colours was available and this one is finished in Ivory. The cabriolets had a different range of six colours.

Main picture - The 356 Speedster of 1954 (at the rear) pictured with a 356A coupé of 1956 vintage. The Speedster made a big impact on the American market, even though sales figures were low.

A 356 1500 cabriolet from 1954.

Left - The interior of a 1956 356A coupé; the quality of materials and finish was very high indeed.

An early 356A coupé photographed in Stuttgart.

A Wendler-bodied 550 Spyder of 1954 (only the first five prototypes had Weidenhausen bodies). This racing car followed the layout of Porsche Number One and helped establish the Porsche legend.

Most of the world-famous Speedsters were 356A models, like this 1956 example. A number were used for racing due to their lower weight.

The legendary Carrera road car - this is a 1956 356A Carrera 1500GS coupé. The Carrera name was adopted in celebration of Porsche's achievements in the great Mexican race.

Right - The 718 RSK Spyder was a highly-successful development of the 550. The 718 itself was later developed into a world class sports car and even a Grand Prix machine.

The Speedster was replaced by this model, the Convertible D, in 1958. This is a very early example as it has "Speedster D" badges (the car was not known by that name after its launch).

A 356B with the rare Karmann hardtop, introduced in August 1960. The Karmann hardtop was to be a shortlived model.

Left - The 356B was launched at the 1959 Frankfurt Show. This is the coupé model.

A 356B cabriolet in a suitably majestic setting.

356 B

F

Le Hardtop
est un des cadets et en même temps un des modèles les plus populaires
de la maison Porsche. La possibilité de rouler à l'air libre en été et à
l'abri en hiver, assurant ainsi le même confort que celui que présente
le coupé, a conduit ce modèle à un succès rapide, modèle caractérisé
par les grandes surfaces de ses glaces et ses montants étroits.

Le Cabriolet
est d'une beauté exquise et offre par son équipement intérieur harmo-
nieux, par le raffinement des tons riches et de bon goût, un confort qui
ne laisse plus rien à désirer. La voiture se transforme en hiver sans
peine en un coupé aux lignes heureuses, grâce à un Hardtop facile
à placer.

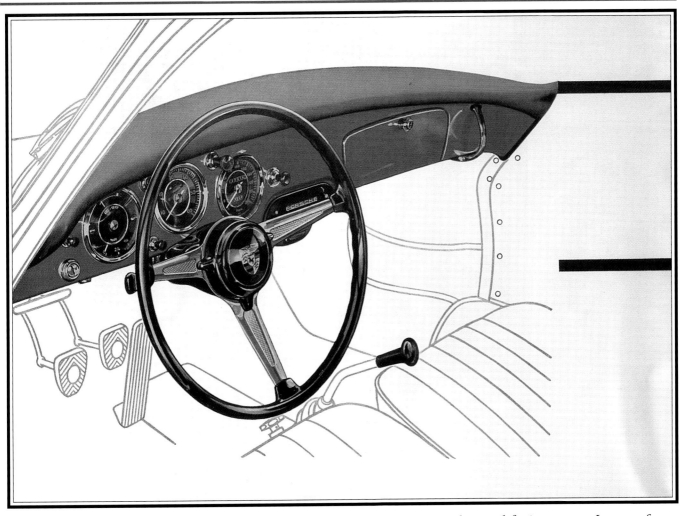

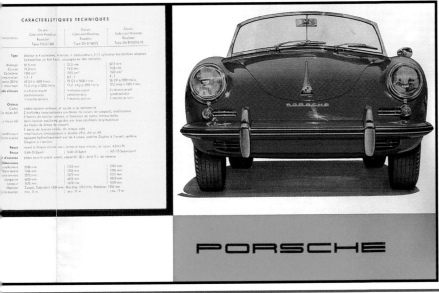

This and facing page - Images from the 1960 French market 356B sales brochure, including "Le Hardtop," "Le Cabriolet" and "Le Roadster."

The Roadster, brought in at the launch of the 356B to replace the Convertible.

Based on the 356B, the Abarth-Carrera with lightweight coachwork by Zagato was perhaps the ultimate development of the pure 356.

This is the 1964 model year cabriolet. The 356C was the last of the 356 line, which was in production officially from 1948 to 1965 (though ten cars like this were built for the Dutch police in 1966!)

In July 1963 Porsche introduced the disc-braked 356C. This is the coupé model.

Without doubt, the 904 was very different to the 356 road cars, but it owed a lot to its ancestry - customer 904s were supplied with the same Carrera engine, for instance.

5

THE 356B

On the 9 September 1959 a new Porsche model was announced. The T-5 (design studies for the T-3 and T-4 body modifications had been rejected) made its public debut at the 1959 Frankfurt Show and, distinguished by the higher position of the headlights in a new wing-line (to conform to regulations in all of the American States), this latest model was given the designation Porsche 356B.

356B features included higher and stronger bumpers front and rear "for better protection against Detroit cars." The air intakes next to the front indicator were modified to look smoother and quarterlights were now standard on the coupé. The floorpan was changed to provide more room for the rear passengers and the rear seat was now a two-piece affair.

The standard 1.6 litre 60bhp 616/1 engine of the 356A was retained, as was the 616/2 Super engine, although the latter was now known as the Super 75 to differentiate it from the new 616/7 Super 90 engine. This 90bhp unit was available from March 1960 and was considered powerful enough to render a Carrera model unnecessary. There was, therefore, no Carrera listed in the Porsche catalogues.

The Super 90 featured a single-leaf transverse compensating spring under the swing axles to reduce rear roll and to diminish oversteer. All models were slightly heavier, but gained an improved

The shortlived Roadster, this Super 90 version being an exhibit in the Porsche Museum.

Type 741 synchromesh, radial tyres and a better braking system developed from the racing programme - different friction linings were used and there were 72 light alloy ribs on the drums to dissipate heat more readily.

The 356B was initially listed with three body styles. The Convertible D was renamed the Roadster, and production for 1959 remained at Drauz. The coupé (built by Reutter at 5000DM each for Porsche), and the cabriolet made up the range. There were seven standard colours offered, plus four optional shades at extra cost. In 1959, prices started at 12,650DM on the home market and from $3580 in America.

Options for the 356B included a special three-piece luggage set, luggage straps, ski or luggage racks, a steel sunroof, a detachable steel hardtop for the cabriolet, leather seats, foglamps, removable headlight grilles, driver's mirror, seatbelts, chrome-plated wheels with knock-off hubs, a choice of radios (either AM or AM/FM), headrests and a tonneau cover for the cabriolet.

Production Highlights
During 1956, 747 workers built 4285 cars and, two years later, 966 people built almost 6000 vehicles. By 1960, Porsche had over 1200 employees and turnover was around 90,000,000DM for the year. A third factory (*Werk III*) was built at Zuffenhausen towards the end of 1959 to cope with the workload.

Exports had risen sharply, from 25 per cent in 1951 to about 70 per cent of production in 1960. In December 1959, Vasek Polak of California opened the first Porsche only showroom in America. The marque already had a countrywide network of service schools to cater for Porsche racers and their mechanics.

With the Drauz contract coming to an end, production of the Roadster moved to D'Ieteren of Brussels in 1960. Reutter, soon to be taken over by Porsche, continued to build bodies and Karmann of Osnabrück built the hardtop coupé (introduced in August 1960).

In fact, both the Roadster and Karmann Hardtop were dropped in June 1962, but Karmann carried on with normal coupé production afterwards. In 1962, Porsche completed its 50,000th car - a 356B cabriolet.

The British Market
In a recent *Classic Cars* Group Test, Brian Palmer noted that the 356B Super 75 Cabriolet had "a carved-from-solid feel." This is indeed quite a compliment, for even for today's convertible car makers, scuttle shake is a problem which is very hard to resolve. Other people in the test praised the car for its

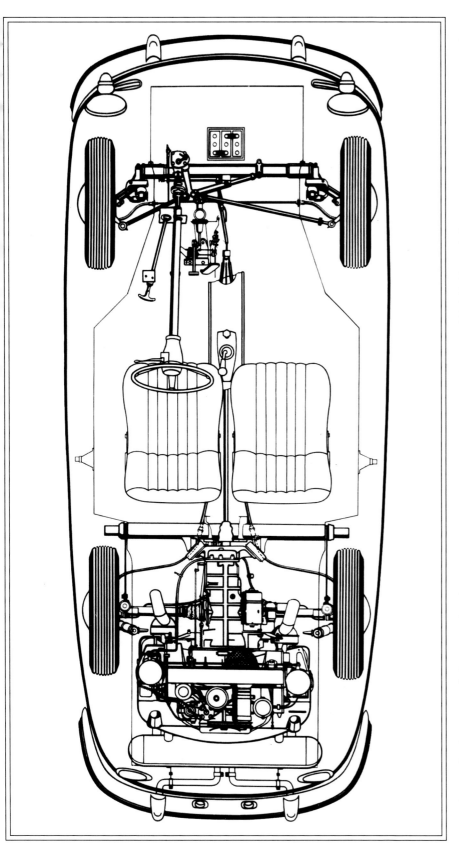

The basic layout of the 356B shown here, was virtually unchanged from that of the original model.

driver appeal, it being described as "charismatic."

However, the Porsche was still rare in Britain, as its price put many people off. In May 1960, the prices of the Porsche range were as follows:

Standard Fixed-head Coupé
            - £2049.12s.6d
Standard Detachable Hardtop
            - £2232.7s.6d
Standard Cabriolet
            - £2296.2s.6d
Super 90 Roadster
            - £2358.9s.2d
Super 90 Fixed-head Coupé
            - £2409.9s.2d
Super 90 Cabriolet
            - £2657.7s.6d

At the same time, a Karmann Ghia was priced at £1166, or a convertible Renault Floride would have cost just £25 more than the Volkswagen. Even the semi-exotic Alfa Romeo Giulietta Spider was cheaper than almost all of the Porsche range at £2090.

Meanwhile, British sports cars were in a different price league. The Triumph TR3 started at just £991, or there was the Austin-Healey 3000 at £1168. Moving upmarket, the Daimler SP250 was £1395, while the Jaguar XK150 started at £1665 - both of the latter cars were substantially faster than the Super 90s, let alone the 356s equipped with the standard 1600 engine.

A Super 75 coupé was tested in 1960 and a 0-60mph time of 11.4

The 50,000th German-built Porsche, leaving the line on 3 April 1962.

An elegant 1960 Beutler-bodied four-seater 356B. The ideal option for the Porsche enthusiast with a family, but very few were sold.

seconds was recorded. The top speed was quoted as being 109mph, but overall fuel consumption over 1114 miles was an exceptional 29.2mpg. The Super 90 cabriolet covered the 0-60 test in 9.7 seconds, and went on to 110mph. Considering that the open cars were slower at the top end than the aerodynamic coupés, this was quite impressive.

Beutler Specials

Beutler had been involved with Porsche from the very beginning,

having built the first Porsche convertibles over the Winter of 1948/49. At the Geneva Show of 1957, a four-seater coupé with a lengthened VW floorpan and Porsche mechanicals was exhibited. It went on sale alongside a convertible version later that year, but only twenty or so cars were sold over the next couple of years. A revised model, again available as a coupé or cabriolet, appeared in 1960. It looked remarkably like the recently-introduced Sunbeam Alpine and proved relatively successful.

At about the same time, a true four-seater 356 was marketed by Beutler. Built on a lengthened 356 floorpan (18 inches was added under the front seats), all of the aluminium panels were unique to Beutler, as was the window glass. Bumpers, all exterior handles, engine cover grilles, tail lights and trim details, however, all came from the standard 356. Although much bigger, the Beutler was about the same weight as a standard car due to the light alloy panels. Around ten four-seater coupés were built between 1958 and 1961 and a couple of cabriolets. If this figure seems low, in 1960 the Beutler-bodied car cost 20,000DM, which goes a long way to explaining why so few were built.

Competition News

Ferry Porsche once said: "Prior to a motor race a certain number of problems have to be solved because otherwise the other manufacturers would win. This impulse is exceedingly important for progress and particularly the quick progress of engineering. It should not be said that ours is an exceptional position because we only build cars that have a sporting tendency and which bear an obvious relationship to sporting success. We also design for other companies and our experience drawn from sports cars in this manner also bears fruit in other designs."

The Carrera had been dropped when the Super 90 arrived; however, in 1960 Reutter built forty lightweight Carrera coupés featuring bucket seats, plexiglass side windows, bigger fuel tanks and better braking. For track use only, they gave between 125bhp and 135bhp depending on the exhaust system.

To meet the ever-increasing threat from Alfa Romeo and Lotus, Porsche exploited the FIA rules to their limits and had a new Carrera made ready to keep their position at the top of the 1600 Class. Around 25 chassis were reserved by Porsche for the Abarth-Carrera project, although eventually only 20 were built (the final chassis number 11021, was 11019 rebuilt).

Wendler (who made the Porsche Spyder bodies) were asked to quote on new lightweight bodies, as were Zagato through Carlo Abarth. Carlo Abarth was married to Anton Piech's secretary and, with Rodolfo Hruska, was the Porsche representative in Italy. It was Abarth who had brought the Cisitalia project to Gmünd.

Zagato of Milan won the contract, but wanted their name kept off the machine, presumably because of their close links with Porsche's competitors Alfa Romeo and Lancia. Designed by Franco Scaglione and built by Zagato, the Abarth badge appeared on the body's flanks.

Porsche shipped 356B (T-5) chassis to Italy, which were then modified by Zagato and the bodies fitted before the assemblies were sent to Stuttgart for the Competition Department to fit the mechanical components. The body was narrower and 5 inches lower than a standard 356B; it was also some 100lb lighter.

The Abarth-Carrera (also known as the GTL or 695GS) had the 1.6 plain bearing engine with repositioned distributors (as introduced in 1958) a higher compression ratio, Weber carburettors and 12v electrics.

Porsche considered the quality of Zagato's workmanship in these cars to be poor but, nevertheless, four or five were made ready for works drivers in 1960. Class wins came at Le Mans (Linge and Walter were the top Porsche finishers in 1960), in the Targa Florio (with Strahle and Linge) and at Sebring and the Nürburgring.

For the 1961 season, the en-

5^{éme} TOUR DE CORSE 1960

Paul Strahle and Herbert Linge on their way to outright victory on the 1960 Tour de Corse, held over four days from 5 November.

gine was given a stronger bottom end and new camshafts. Now developing 128bhp at 6700rpm (or 135bhp at 7400rpm with the straight-through Sebring exhaust), good results followed in the Targa Florio (another Class win) and at Le Mans where Herbert Linge and Ben Pol took tenth place in their works-entered 695GS. In the same race the Buchet/Monneret machine, in the French racing colours, retired with engine failure just one hour from the end; it had been lying in 12th position. Hans Joachim Walter (sometimes known as Heini) won the Hillclimb title in 1961 and was later given the use of a larger 1.7 litre works' engine.

On the rally scene, with more modest machinery, Boutin and Motte won the 1960 Lyon-Charbonnieres Rally outright and, in the Tour de Corse of the same

Cutaway 356 (T-6) built for the motor show circuit in 1961. The eagle-eyed will spot the new dished steering wheel introduced in 1959 (a wood rim was optional).

year, the Strahle/Linge pairing won in a Super 90 - Gerard Larrouse (of Formula One fame) repeated the marque's success on the event in 1969.

The Last Major Change

At the Frankfurt Show in September 1961, the T-6 body made its debut. There were a number of new features to distinguish the latest model, such as the larger front and rear windows on the coupé, a new engine cover with two grilles fitted across the range and a larger front

Below - The differences between the T-5 (left) and T-6 body styles can clearly be seen in this photograph - at the rear the T-6 had a larger back window and twin grilles on a lower engine cover.

MotorSport : "In practice, the Porsche does oversteer in quite a big way, but the experienced driver, having entered a corner at speed, allows the steering to unwind as the turn is negotiated, which can be a smooth and effortless operation."

The Super 90 cabriolet was priced at £2876 2s 9d after taxes. One magazine commented: "The new Porsche, and particularly the Super 90, has reached such an incredibly high state of development that it would seem very difficult, if not impossible, to improve it materially."

Indeed, the standard road cars hardly changed at all after this point, except for the adoption of disc brakes. As *Motor* pointed out: "It is amazing that it still has so few competitors or imitators."

However, the Carrera 2 was quite a different beast.

The Carrera 2

At the same time as the T-6 356B was introduced, the Carrera returned to the line-up. Named the Carrera 2, it had a two litre 130bhp version of the traditional Carrera engine and was sold to the public from April 1962 onwards.

Carrera 2 introduced disc brakes to the Porsche marque (fitted from April 1962, when sales began, despite having been announced at Frankfurt with drum brakes), although the rest of the range would have to wait. These early disc brakes were of a Porsche

hood featuring a squarer-shaped leading edge (which in turn led to more luggage space).

An electrically-operated sunroof was offered as an option and air intake louvres were added to the front scuttle for improved ventilation. In addition, the fuel filler was placed in the right-hand front wing on lhd cars and the cabriolet rear window gained a zip to enable its removal. Mechanically, there was a more efficient oil cooler and the Super 90 now used cast-iron cylinders (like the stand-

ard 1600) and was fitted with a beefier clutch. Both the Roadster and Karmann Hardtop were dropped from the range in June 1962, by which time prices had risen by nearly 10 per cent since the introduction of the 356B.

The Super 75 coupé was listed in Britain at £2348 (including Purchase Tax) at this time and was capable of 0-60mph in either 11.9 or 13.5 seconds, depending on which magazine one reads, with a top speed in the region of 108mph.

William Boddy noted in

The Carrera returns; this is a Carrera 2 homologation car.

Engine bay of the two-litre Carrera 2. The Carrera 2 2000GS had a skirt under the rear bumper through which the exhaust pipes exited.

design, as opposed to the Ate units fitted later and, in all honesty, were not the best design to come from Stuttgart. However, only 100 cars were planned for homologation purposes and, by the time that the Ate brakes were standard on the 356C version, this figure had easily been surpassed.

Bill Boddy of *MotorSport* , despite the fact that he only had the car for a very short time, thought the Carrera 2 was "a truly sensa-

The 2000GS/GT (or Dreikantschaber) at the Nürburgring.

Le Mans 1962. Car 35 (entered by Veuillet) was driven by Buchet and Schiller to 12th overall, while car 34 finished five places higher in the hands of Edgar Barth and Hans Herrmann - enough to take a Class victory.

tional GT car, docile in top gear, with a surprisingly quiet and flexible engine."

Motor magazine echoed these sentiments by saying: "Even more impressive, however, is the extent to which the complex Carrera engine has been civilized in this latest version. It is extremely flexible and accelerates very strongly from low rpm without any flat spots and with no steps in the power curve."

With 130bhp on tap from the 1996cc engine, *Auto Motor und Sport* tested a Carrera 2 GS in 1962, and recorded a top speed of 124mph and a 0-60 (actually 62mph, as the German magazine uses 100kph as its yardstick) time of 8.6 seconds. Another magazine managed 127mph, but for around $7600 one would have been forgiven for expecting nothing less. In all, 310 of the 356B Carrera 2s were built.

More Motorsport Success

For 1962, works engines on the Abarth-Carrera had around 140bhp with special pistons. There was a Class win and 7th overall at Sebring for Dan Gurney and Bob Holbert, a Class win at the Nürburgring, and good results once again in the Targa Florio and at Le Mans.

The only Porsche representatives at Le Mans were three 1.6 litre 695GS models, two entered by the works, and one by Veuillet. The works car of Barth/Herrmann took seventh overall and a Class win,

The 2000GS/GT at the Porsche works in 1963.

while the French machine driven by Buchet and Schiller came 12th. The other works' car retired early on.

In 1963, GTLs were placed fifth and seventh in the Daytona Continental. Most GTLs were given 140bhp two litre engines and disc brakes later in their lives. The cost of a GTL was very high at 25,000DM,

but one had achieved no less than 138mph on the Mulsanne Straight at Le Mans, so perhaps the GTL was worth the money!

However, for the 1963 season, two prototype vehicles (known as the 2000GS/GT model, or *Dreikantschaber*, at the factory) had been built on modified 356B chassis with aluminium alloy bodies: it was later decided glassfibre would be easier material to use for future racing car bodies. The rather strange window arrangement of these cars was designed to overcome the Le Mans organiser's feelings that there wasn't enough glass in the car to make it a GT. Power was between 155bhp and 180bhp.

At Sebring in 1963, the 2000GS/GT models came 9th and 10th overall (first and second in Class) and in the Targa Florio, Edgar

A gathering of Porsche fans in Tokyo after a parade through Ginza. Huschke von Hanstein had won the GT Class at the 1963 Japanese Grand Prix in the same week.

356B Chassis Numbers

The chassis numbers of the 356B models are listed below. Also included are the racing cars directly based upon the 356B, such as the Abarth-Carrera.

T-5 body -

1959 coupé	108918 to 110237
1959 cabriolet	152476 to 152943
1959 Roadster	86831 to 87391
1960 coupé	110238 to 112990
	and 112993 to 114650
1960 cabriolet	152944 to 154560
1960 Roadster	87392 to 88920
1961 coupé	114651 to 117476
1961 Karmann h/top	200001 to 201048
1961 cabriolet	154561 to 155569
1961 Roadster	88921 to 89483

T-6 body -

1961 coupé	117601 to 118950
1961 Karmann h/top	201601 to 202200
1961 cabriolet	155601 to 156200
1961 Roadster	89601 to 89800
1962 coupé	118951 to 123042
	and 210001 to 210899
1962 Karmann h/top	202201 to 202299
1962 cabriolet	156201 to 156999
	and 157000 to 157768
1962 Karmann coupé	210900 to 212171
1963 coupé	123043 to 125239
1963 Karmann coupé	212172 to 214400
1963 cabriolet	157769 to 158700

Racing cars -

Abarth-Carrera	11001 to 11021
2000 GS/GT	112991 to 112992

Barth and Herbert Linge took the 2000GS/GT to third place. At Le Mans, disaster struck with the two GT cars leaving the event early after engine trouble.

Dickie Stoop was well-known in British club-racing circles, having driven Cooper single-seaters and being noted for great race successes with his Carreras. He bought a Carrera 2 in July 1963 and later a 904 (which he also used on the road!) At Snetterton in England, Dickie Stoop won the GT Class in his old Carrera in 1961 and again in 1963. He also won the Spa 500km Race in 1963, proving his top class quality as a driver.

In rallying during 1962, the GT Class went to Porsche drivers in the Monte Carlo Rally, the Lyon-Charbonnieres event and the Tulip Rally. In addition, Heini Walter won a Coupé des Alpes. In the 1963 Rally of the Midnight Sun, Berndt Jansson won in his Carrera 2 and in the Tulip Rally of the same year, Bakker and Umbach won the GT Class in a Super 90 - the Touring Class was won by Greder/Delalande in a Ford Falcon Sprint.

6

BUILDING THE MOTORSPORT LEGEND

In the 1950s Porsche, EMW and Borgward from Germany, Maserati and its close-cousin the OSCA from Italy and the Cooper and Lotus teams of England provided the crowds with some exciting racing in the 1 litre Class. EMW was actually the East German branch of BMW, but the marque had disappeared by 1955 and their cars only raced outside Europe once.

The Borgward name came about when Carl Borgward bought the Goliath and Hansa-Lloyd concerns in the late 1920s. From 1939, he amalgamated his various companies to form Borgward but, despite some heavy involvement in motorsport, never really used his track successes to promote a sports car, deciding instead to concentrate on saloons and coupés.

The Maserati brothers built the first car to bear their name in 1926, although the family had been involved with the Italian motor in-

The 550A had a lighter (1170lb against 1215lb) but stiffer spaceframe chassis. Wendler did the coachwork which, as can be seen in the photograph, was of very high quality for a racing car.

dustry almost since its birth. In 1947, they left the Maserati concern to form OSCA (which had faded away by 1967) but the Maserati marque continued trading under Adolfo Orsi, who had bought the Modena company some ten years earlier.

The Cooper Car Company had come a long way and was now a force to be reckoned with in both the sports racing and Grand Prix circles. Cooper won the Formula One Championship in 1959 and 1960. Lotus was the dream of Colin Chapman. His cars were delicate (perhaps too delicate sometimes), but very quick due to superior chassis design and lightness.

Baron Fritz Huscke von Hanstein was Porsche's Racing Team Manager and Wilhelm Hild was the head of the Racing Department. The racing shop was separate from the main assembly hall and for a period drivers were engaged race by race. However, it was already a professional outfit, further enhanced by the arrival of a new model - the 550A.

The 550A

In 1956, the Wendler-bodied 550A was introduced. Gone was the ladder chassis of the old Spyder, replaced by a lighter but stiffer spaceframe which incorporated a low-pivot swing axle rear suspension like the Mercedes. A new five-speed gearbox with a low first for quicker starts was fitted, the fuel tank was enlarged, and there were wider brake drums for greater efficiency. The 550A used the old 1500RS designation to confuse historians!

The 1956 Mille Miglia (which started on 29 April) saw the debut of the 135bhp 550A (the first 550A models used the 547/2 version of the Carrera engine) but, sadly, it was to retire. In fact, it was a poor showing generally by Porsche's previous standards in the event, with only the 356s taking Class honours to save some face.

Wolfgang von Trips and Umberto Maglioli drove to fourth overall (and a Class win) in the Nürburgring 1000km Race, held in May. The infamous Micheal May winged car was at this event and it was actually Von Hanstein who protested and had it disqualified - Mays' Porsche was faster than the works machines. Amazingly, nobody followed up this brilliant piece of aerodymanics until more than a decade later.

For the 1956 Targa Florio, only one 550A, hastily painted white, was sent along together with two

Left - The 550A coupé that Von Frankenberg and Von Trips took to fifth in the 1956 Le Mans 24-hour Race.

Claude Storez being chased by a Ferrari at Le Mans in 1957.

mechanics. The event was won outright by Umberto Maglioli and the 550A (at 56.85mph). Maglioli had given Porsche their first taste of victory on the Targa Florio; he would go on to compete in a total of 19 Targas between 1948 and 1970. Only one man in the history of the race bettered that distinction, Mantia Sergio, who started in 1920.

At Le Mans, apart from the Von Frankenberg/Von Trips 550A (with a coupé body as full windscreens were required) which took fifth overall, the Stuttgart concern had only one other finisher out of six entries, and this was a 356A. The weather could be blamed for the poor results, but the reality was that the other 550A had piston trouble and the two earlier 550 Spyders also succumbed to mechanical problems.

Other 1956 races on French soil included the Paris 1000km Race, in which the company gained a Class victory and there was a Porsche one, two, three in the Reims 12-hour event.

On the final Mille Miglia, beginning 12 May 1957, Maglioli took fifth overall (only 47 minutes behind the winning Ferrari of Taruffi) and a Class win in the 1500cc Sports category. The 356 of Strahle/ Linge came away with a Class win in the 1600cc GT listing.

There was a Class win at the Nürburgring 1000km Race for Maglioli and Barth, and for the first time the public got to see the prototype Porsche 718 RS. By now, the

cars were producing 142bhp from the 547/3 engine.

At the 1957 Le Mans 24-hour Race, out of six starters, only one Porsche finished, and that was a private entry. Driven by Hugus and de Beaufort, the 550A came in in eighth place and won the 1500cc Class. The only other point of interest was the appearance of the 718 RS (chassis 718-001), driven by Umberto Maglioli and Edgar Barth. The car was lighter and had larger brakes than the 550A and was said

to be very quick before it retired halfway through the event.

The 718 RSK

The one-off Type 645 served as the prototype for the 718. The 645's first race came at Solitude in July 1956, where it came fourth despite a number of problems. Its second outing, at the Berlin Grand Prix in September, was to be its last. It veered off the circuit on the notorious banking and was destroyed in a ball of flames but,

"Mickey Mouse" which had an oil cooler on the body and magnesium alloy panels. It was destroyed in an accident on 16 September 1956.

Below - Wolfgang von Trips on the Lenzerheide hillclimb in 1957. He was testing the 1.7 litre Carrera engine on the event.

Bottom - The 718 RSK prototype, seen here at Le Mans in 1957.

fortunately, Richard von Frankenberg was thrown free beforehand and could count himself lucky to be alive. Von Frankenberg called the car "Mickey Mouse" because he said it described the handling and braking.

The 718 prototype was built up over the winter of 1956/57. It was an even lighter machine, built around a spaceframe and some 5 inches lower than the old 550 Spyder. An improved suspension, superior braking through the use of turbofinned brake drums and 142bhp (increased to 148bhp by 1959) resulted in a far better car. The 718 RS became the 718 RSK via suspension changes - these were later reverted to original specification - but the RSK name stayed.

In 1957, the European Hillclimb Championship was revived, with a maximum engine capacity of 2 litres. Porsche used the championship to test larger engines (with capacities of 1587cc and 1679cc) based on the Type 547 in preparation for the RSK. At the first round on Mont Ventoux, Barth and Maglioli competed in a 1.5 litre Spyder. In the second round at Freiburg, a 1.6 Spyder was seen for the first time with improved torque and 148bhp on tap. By the fourth round at Lenzerheide, there was a 1.7 Spyder for Von Trips and the prototype RSK for Von Frankenberg. These power-units would later appear in a number of works-backed machines in various events.

Porsche for the 1957 Reims F2 Race, held in July.

Unfortunately, the RSK never made it to Reims, as it was written off by Umberto Maglioli at Le Mans three weeks earlier after hitting Tony Brooks' Aston Martin. Instead, Christian Goethals was left to represent the marque by entering a privately-owned 550 Spyder. After qualifying eighth, he moved up three places to finish fifth overall in the race.

Two 550A Spyders were entered by the works for the Nürburgring Grand Prix event, driven by Maglioli and Edgar Barth. The latter, despite being relatively new in the Porsche camp (he was still contracted to Borgward at the time), took advantage of his knowledge of the course and won the F2 Class. Count Carel Godin de Beaufort took third in Class in his private 550A Spyder, while Maglioli failed to finish.

The RSK made only two appearances at the race track in the 1957 season. At the Nürburgring in May (its debut) it was taken out for practice, but didn't take the starter's flag. In the following month, it was at Le Mans. However, 1957 was to be the last year for the works 550As.

Competition in 1958
In January 1958, Stirling Moss and Jean Behra came third overall in the Buenos Aires 1000km Race. Moss should have driven a Maserati, but the car was damaged

Formula 2 also returned in 1957 after a couple of seasons in the wilderness, but there was no officially recognised Championship anywhere other than in Britain. New regulations dictated that 1.5 litre engines running on pump fuel would form the basis for the Formula Two cars of 1957. Von Hanstein considered that the RSK would be suitable (it actually needed very little modification) and entered

to third place overall.

A race at Zeltweg Airfield in Austria, August 1958. Ernst Vogel is nearest the camera in the 550A, with Edgar Barth (in the middle) and Jean Behra driving the 718 RSKs. The event was won by Von Trips, with Behra second and Barth third.

before the race, so Von Hanstein offered him a drive in a 1.6 litre 550A. It was the last time that the company relied solely on the old model.

By early 1958, the definitive 718 RSK had arrived. The K-style front suspension was dispensed with, replaced by the original set-up. At the rear, a pair of Watts linkages was used and coil springs were used in place of the old torsion bars. Experiments had been carried out in 1958 with "Jet Cooling" (introduced by Fletcher Aviation on their Jeep) as a possible replacement for the power-sapping dual-entry fan, but were not adopted. Wishbones and coil springs were used at the rear on the works' cars for 1959.

At the 1958 Sebring 12-hour event, the Schell/Seidel pairing came third overall, just seven laps down on the winners. Jean Behra and Giorgio Scarlatti came second on the Targa Florio, winning their Class in the process. They used a finned 718 RSK; fins had first been

seen at Le Mans in 1957 and some drivers swore by them, others swore at them!

At the 1958 Le Mans 24-hour Race, Behra and Herrmann took their 1.6 litre 718 RSK to third place overall and victory in the two litre Class - the sister car was the only Porsche to retire. The 1.5 litre 718 RSK of Edgar Barth and Paul Frere came fourth, while the two 550As entered took fifth and sixth places.

Count Wolfgang Berghe von Trips started racing private Porsches before moving up to a works' drive. Born in 1928, his promising career was cut short in 1961 when his Ferrari F1 car crashed - he died, taking fourteen spectators with him. However, during 1958, he won two hillclimbs outright for Porsche and was declared the European Hill Climb Champion.

Competition in 1959

Borgward withdrew from racing in the early part of 1959, so Porsche won the European Hillclimb

The loss of Jean Behra was felt by everyone in motorsport. The main characters in this 1958 picture are Huschke von Hanstein (white jumper), Wolfgang von Trips (with camera), Jean Behra (in the car) and Edgar Barth on the far right.

Below - Detail shot of the central-seater Porsche RSK.

Championship easily through ex-Borgward star Edgar Barth - he took five overall victories to clinch the title. Apart from Barth, Borgward also had Jo Bonnier and Hans Herrmann in the team, but they were in serious financial trouble and soon afterwards the company was sold to the Government.

In the meantime, the Sesslar/ Holbert pairing took a Class victory in the 1959 Sebring 12-hour Race, actually finishing ahead of the works' car driven by Von Trips and Bonnier. Shortly after, Von Dory and Mieres won at Daytona.

On the 1959 Targa Florio, Edgar Barth and Wolfgang Seidel delivered Porsche's second victory in the classic event. They averaged 57.07mph and also took the fastest lap. Behind them was a trio of Porsche drivers; Mahle finishing second, Strahle and Linge third, with local man Pucci and Von Hanstein coming in fourth. The last time a German driver had won was in 1924, when the Mercedes-Benz that won had been modified by Professor Porsche.

The Targa was the highlight in a season of mixed fortunes but, before the disasters, the Nürburgring 1000km Race again saw Porsches filling the first four places.

At Le Mans, all six Porsches entered (five 718 RSKs and a 550 RS) failed to finish. A different camshaft had been tried on the works cars, but obviously the advantages

on paper were heavily outweighed by the disadvantages in reality.

Jean Behra died in his RSK at AVUS. Born in 1921, his racing career had spanned about a decade. Fortunately, De Beaufort was luckier than Behra, for having gone over the AVUS banking as well, his car landed on its wheels and, amazingly, continued the race! Hans Herrmann was lucky to survive an horrific crash in the BRM he drove in the German Grand Prix the next day, bringing an awful weekend to

118

*The open-wheeled 718/2
Formula Two car of 1959.*

a close.

On a brighter note, the Swiss driver, Heini Walter, was declared the German Sports Car Champion (1500 Class) in 1959 driving a private RSK. RSKs also had a superb 1959 SCCA season with Ken Miles, Jack McAfee, Don Sesslar and Bob Holbert. The 1960 SCCA Class F Sports Champion was Roger Penske in a 718 RSK.

By now, the 1.5 litre engine was producing around 150bhp at 7800rpm (547/3), while the 1.6 litre version (547/4) put out 160bhp and the 1.7 Type 547/5 gave 170bhp. The 1.7 litre engine had been seen in both the Targa Florio and the Tourist Trophy at Goodwood in 1959.

Specials

Wim Poll, the son of the VW dealer from Hilversum in Holland, was a real Porsche fanatic and was very successful in racing. As well as competing with a 356 Carrera, in 1956 he had the "Poll-Platje" Spyder built: it was fitted with a 1300S engine. Poll was later offered a 1.6 litre engine from the works, enabling him to take his National Championship on a number of occasions.

The Hirondelle Spyder was built by Henke van Zalinge in 1957 and was powered by a 1.6 litre Carrera engine (later replaced by a Super 90 unit). The car was raced in Van Zalinge's native Holland for around five years, recording a number of successes at national level.

Ian Frazer-Jones raced a Porsche 1500S-powered Cooper in South Africa during the mid-1950s. Another famous car was the "Pooper" of Peter Lovely (a Volkswagen dealer in Seattle). Seen regularly on the American circuits, this was a modified Cooper 500 machine fitted with a 1500S engine and streamlined body. Johnny von Neumann also had a Cooper with a Porsche engine, as did fellow American Gordon Lipe.

Porsche Single-Seaters

As early as 1953, Ferry Porsche had hinted that Porsche might become involved with Grand Prix racing. In October 1958, the CSI announced that Formula One would run with 1.5 litre cars with a minimum weight of 500kg for 1961. Naturally, this suited Porsche down to the ground, as the engine size was already at its production capacity and the weight would not present any problems.

In the meantime, Porsche continued to field the RSK in Formula Two races. For the 1958 event at Reims, Von Hanstein entered the ex-Barth/Frère RSK that had won its Class at Le Mans. It featured an updated rear suspension and a central driving seat and steering wheel. With an aluminium tonneau cover and rear wheel spats, it

was extremely aerodynamic and, in order to save weight, the spare wheel and lights had been removed. Jean Behra drove the car and won quite easily from Peter Collins in a Ferrari Dino 156.

The car was out again (albeit slightly modified) for the Nürburgring Grand Prix, with Barth taking it to sixth overall and second in Class. It stayed in Germany for the Berlin Grand Prix at AVUS, held in late September. Masten Gregory drove the machine, winning his heat, and then went on to win the F2 Class. The event was won, rather ironically, by Jean Behra in his rather more standard RSK.

Jean Behra was the German Sports Car Champion in 1958 (1500 Class) and commissioned his own F2 single-seater. Built around a Valerio Colotti-designed space-frame chassis, it had originally been a two-seater 718 RSK so Colotti (who was an ex-Maserati man) drew up the new design to accept the RSK mechanical components. As Jean Behra was a Frenchman, he had the "Behra-Porsche" painted in the traditional French racing blue.

At the same time, a programme was instigated so that Porsche would have an open-wheeled F2 car for 1959, using it as a test-bed for the proposed F1 machine for 1961. Wilhelm Hild, Helmut Bott and Hans Mezger developed the car alongside the RSK and even gave it a Type 718/2 designation rather than its own distinct project number.

It was interesting to see other Grand Prix teams advocating what Porsche had always believed - the engine is better off at the back. The Cooper F1 car of 1957 was the final proof, and prompted more to follow. However, one driver remembered the exhaust note of the Porsche Formula racing cars sounding like "ducks fartin' through long grass!"

After Sebring was behind them, Porsche concentrated on the single-seater, and had it running by April 1959. Running modifications found on the works RSKs were employed, but otherwise the car was very much the same as the Type 718 under the skin, save for the new narrow chassis frame and the detail changes that this necessitated.

Testing on the Malmsheim Airfield and then at the Nürburgring in the first week of May, proved to be successful, so the car was entered for the 1959 Monaco Grand Prix.

The True Formula Cars

The Behra F2 car made its debut at Monte Carlo for the 1959 Monaco Grand Prix. However, with Behra contracted to drive for Ferrari, Maria Teresa de Filippis handled the Behra-Porsche, but failed to qualify it. More importantly, the works F2 Porsche was also putting in its first appearance.

Sent unpainted to Monte Carlo (there simply had not been time to spray the body), Von Trips did well in qualifying (getting in amongst the F1 cars) but, unfortunately, crashed the vehicle on the second lap of the race, taking out the Lotus of Bruce Halford and Ferrari of Cliff Allison in the process.

For the Reims event, the single-seater was repaired following its Monaco debacle. Jo Bonnier took third place, behind Stirling Moss (Cooper-Borgward) and the Behra-Porsche, driven on this occasion by Hans Herrmann. Von Trips managed fifth in a works RSK with central steering (chassis 718-007).

In the middle of the season, Behra left the Ferrari camp and, at last, had a chance to drive his own machine in anger. Wolfgang Seidel, Carel Godin de Beaufort and Christian Goethals all had RSKs that were capable of being converted to central cockpit models and these were entered for the 1959 Pau Grand Prix. Also there was the Behra-Porsche which qualified on the front row (this time driven by Behra himself) and a conventional lhd RSK driven by Harry Schell. After leading briefly, Behra could only muster fifth place at the end and Schell finished eighth - the only Porsche finishers.

At the German Grand Prix held at the Avus circuit, Behra entered his Spyder for the sports car race on the day before the Grand Prix and the Behra-Porsche for the main event. Sadly, he never got to drive his F2 car, as the Frenchman lost his life in the Spyder. As a sign of respect, the Porsche team withdrew their entries for the weekend and the Behra-Porsche eventually went to the Camoradi team.

The Behra-Porsche passed to Lloyd Casner and it came 12th in the 1960 Argentine Grand Prix with Masten Gregory at the wheel. Later in the year, in July, it was seen during the practice session of the German Grand Prix, but Herrmann, its driver, later drove a works' car instead. Fred Gamble took 10th at the 1960 Italian Grand Prix, but the Behra-Porsche's best days were well and truly behind it.

In the meantime, the works single-seater gained better coachwork, aimed at improving it with regard to feeding air to the engine and aerodynamically. The car also gained some paint for the first time in its career, but after practice with Von Trips, it was withdrawn from the Avus event as a sign of respect following Behra's fatal accident.

Left - The revised bodywork of the 1959 machine. Note the familiar-looking engine.

Jo Bonnier was sent to Brands Hatch in August, and finished fourth in the Kentish 100 event. Stirling Moss was impressed enough by the German car to test it at Goodwood a week later, with the result that Rob Walker was loaned a works' F2 car for Moss' use for the whole of the 1960 season. The English maestro said "the only bad things about that car were its gearchange and the way it looked!" - nine entries over the year resulted in four victories.

The 1960 Season
Porsche's proper F2 car for 1960 was built on a wheelbase which was 4 inches longer, although it still featured drum brakes. The first car was tested by Herbert Mimler in the wet at Hockenheim in February 1960, after which it was painted blue and white (Rob Walker's colours) and sent to Syracuse for Stirling Moss to use in the F2 race of 19 March. Having qualified on pole, the engine failed in the race.

For 1960, Porsche had given Stirling Moss (the reigning Formula 2 British Champion) the use of the new 718/2 for the whole season, but also signed up Jo Bonnier to campaign a full F2 season for the works. Jo Bonnier, born in Sweden in 1930, competed in sports cars alongside his Grand Prix career. Another man to do that was Graham Hill, who moved over to Porsche sports cars in 1960, but also drove the Stuttgart single-seaters.

Bonnier was first seen at Brussels in April in the second 718/2 alongside Moss, but it was Moss who finished the best - second after the two heats. After an event at Goodwood, the next big race was at Pau. Olivier Gendebien drove the works car, but he complained bitterly about the gearchange and handling. Nonetheless, he still finished third. The first open-wheeled victory for Porsche came on 30 April 1960 when Stirling Moss won the Aintree 200, followed home by Bonnier and Graham Hill to give a Porsche one, two, three.

By July, two more chassis (718204 and 718205) were completed, the latter having a Butzi Porsche styled body with a vastly reduced frontal area and flatter sides. At the German Grand Prix, all five 718s ran in the F2 event. Bonnier won, with Von Trips second, while the three other Porsches were separated only by the Cooper-Climax of Jack Brabham.

After the Solitude Grand Prix defeat on home ground (held a week before the German Grand Prix), Porsche had their revenge by beating Ferrari at Modena a few weeks later - Bonnier won from Ginther and Von Trips.

The Italian Grand Prix (held on 4 September) saw Hans Herrmann qualify tenth on the grid, almost 17 seconds down on pole. However, he finished sixth (three laps behind Phil Hill in the winning Ferrari) to give Porsche their only World Championship point of the 1960 season.

Jack Brabham (Cooper-Climax) was declared Champion, and deservedly so.

To end the year, Moss won the F2 race at Zeltweg Airfield and also the Cape GP and South African GP. Bonnier won at Modena and Hans Herrmann took victory at Innsbruck Airfield. Porsche won the Formula Two Championship.

The 1961 Season
In 1961, Bonnier was joined full-time by the American, Dan Gurney, so that Porsche could launch a full-scale attack in Formula One racing. Gurney, the amiable American, was born in 1931. He had a works drive with the Ferrari sports car team in 1959 and also had a number of F1 drives for the Modena company. Following a bad year with BRM in 1960, he moved to Porsche.

The Type 804 should have made its 1962 debut at Monaco, but it didn't until Zandvoort. The old 718/2 cars therefore started the 1961 season with a coil and wishbone suspension before two new 787s appeared - the first being completed in April. Porsche's F1 debut came at Brussels on 9 April 1961, but they failed to get the desired results.

The second 787 was ready for the Dutch Grand Prix (22 May), but after disappointing results, Ferry Porsche decided to use older 718/2s (the last chassis had been converted into half 718/2, half 787) until the 804 was ready and ordered that the two 787s be scrapped.

Micheal May had moved from Mercedes-Benz in July 1961 and introduced Bosch fuel-injection to the Porsche four-cylinder Grand Prix engine. It increased power by 20bhp, but the idea was dropped and carburettors were retained. In later years, the May head on the V12 Jaguar engine transformed the already-excellent power-unit.

At the end of the 1961 Grand Prix Season, Dan Gurney was fourth (he actually had the same number of points as Stirling Moss in third), with second places in the French, Italian and US Grands Prix. The French Grand Prix was interesting in that it was won by Giancarlo Baghetti in his Formula One debut - nobody else has ever managed this feat before or since. Gurney had led out of the last bend, but Baghetti pulled out of his slipstream to win by a car's length.

Jo Bonnier, despite having set pole on a number of occasions, was well down the field in 15th, but he did at least beat Graham Hill and Roy Salvadori. As a manufacturer, Porsche claimed an easy third, beaten only by the Ferrari and Lotus teams.

As a matter of interest, the 1961 Solitude Grand Prix was a non-Championship race for F1 cars (held 23 July). Porsche had sent three 718s (for Bonnier, Gurney and Herrmann) and a 787 for Barth. Disc brakes were used for the first time - Porsche were actually the last works' cars in F1 to give up on drum brakes - but the event was won by Von Trips in a Ferrari 156.

With the 804 now ready, the old cars were sold off at 50,000DM each, one of them going to Carel Godin de Beaufort, a Dutch Count, one to Heinz Schiller and another to Count Volpi.

The End of Formula Racing

Four 804 Grand Prix cars were built for the 1962 season. The eight-cylinder engine (designed by Hans Mezger and Herr Honich) had gone on test in December 1960 and proved satisfactory. Porsche also developed a special disc brake.

Torsion bar suspension was dropped in favour of wishbones located by longitudinal radius arms.

Most of the leading players had turned to a monocoque chassis by 1963, but for the time being, only the Lotus 25 showed the way forward. At least the Porsche 804 had a frontal area that was some 25 per cent smaller than its predecessor. Side-by-side, the eight-cylinder Type 804 was dwarfed by the original four-cylinder Grand Prix car.

Graham Hill, who had such an awful year with BRM in 1961, was World Champion with them in 1962. Dan Gurney was again Por-

Dan Gurney on his way to victory in the 1962 French Grand Prix. The eight-cylinder Type 804 gave Porsche its only win in a World Championship event.

Below - The elegant lines of the RS60 Spyder.

sche's top man, finishing fifth after a win in the French Grand Prix (at Rouen on 8 July), a third at the Nürburgring and a fifth place in his native country. He also won a minor event at the Solitude circuit with the eight-cylinder car, followed home on that occasion by his team mate Bonnier (a third car had been entered for Jo Siffert).

At the end of the season, Bonnier was again well down the field with three Championship points, only one more than the privateer C.G. de Beaufort in his earlier machines. However, combining the totals gave Porsche fifth place in the Manufacturers' Championship.

Dan Gurney's victory in the French Grand Prix was to be Porsche's only win in a World Championship event. Formula One proved to be too expensive and, despite having invested a small fortune in developing the flat-eight engine, it was decided to cut the company's losses and withdraw from the Grand Prix circus.

At the end of the 1962 season, Von Hanstein announced that Porsche was withdrawing from the world of Formula One to concentrate their efforts on endurance racing and the European Hillclimb Championship. The official reason for their withdrawal was that Ferry Porsche felt that the Formula cars were too far removed from production machines for Porsche owners to identify with.

Thanks to privateers, 1963 was the last time the Porsche marque appeared in the World Championship. Mitter took fourth in the German Grand Prix and De Beaufort managed sixth in both the Belgian and US Grands Prix. In all, this gave five points, and seventh place to Porsche as a constructor. To put this into perspective, the winning Lotus team finished with 54, followed by BRM on 36. Sadly, De Beaufort died following an accident during practice for the 1964 German Grand Prix at the Nürburgring.

Back to Sports Cars - the RS60

The RS60 had a larger windscreen than the old RSK to meet the new FIA regulations for 1960. These rules also stipulated that a car should have luggage space - after trying to make enough room under the front hood, a compartment was later mounted above the gearbox at the back. Otherwise, the RS60 was basically similar to the 718, except for the slightly longer wheelbase (plus 4 inches) and the fact that the 1.7 litre engine was now pumping out 180bhp. Wendler continued to build the bodies.

The first race of the Sports Car Championship was won by Phil Hill in a Ferrari, but Gendebien

The four works-entered Porsches that campaigned the Le Mans 24-hour Race (there were also two private entries). Nearest the camera is the Abarth-Carrera of Linge and Walter, while behind it are three RS60 Spyders. Number 39 was the only RS60 to finish the event.

Heini Walter at the startline of the Freiburg hillclimb in 1961. He was European Hill Climb Champion in 1960 and 1961 driving this RS60.

and Herrmann took overall victory in the Sebring 12-hour Race, beating a gaggle of Ferraris to the flag.

Roger Penske took a Class win at Watkins Glen in a non-Championship event and then Jo Bonnier and Hans Herrmann won the Targa Florio. Winning at an average of 59.58mph, they also took the fastest lap. Edgar Barth and Graham Hill won the 1600 Sports Class.

At the Nürburgring 1000km Race (also in May), the Bonnier/Gendebien pairing came second in an RS60 (first in Class) behind Moss and Gurney in a Maserati Tipo 61. This left only Le Mans to finish off the Championship.

The new decade signified a period of Ferrari dominance in the event, and it was Ferrari's results in the 24-hour Race that sealed the title for them. Just two of the six Porsches entered finished, the best placing coming from the Abarth-Carrera of Linge and Walter (sixth overall and a Class win). The only other car of the marque to complete the course was the RS60 of Barth and Seidel. The RS60 was 11th overall after it lost three of its five gears. In any case, Porsche could be proud of their second place in

the Championship.

Heini Walter was declared the 1960 European Hill Climb Champion driving the RS60, a feat that he repeated in 1961.

The RS61

The RS61 was virtually the same as the RS60, although there were one or two special vehicles built on the chassis, such as the eight-cylinder Grand Prix-engined car. The Camoradi team from America was works supported for the whole of the 1961 season and Scuderia Venezia was works supported on the Targa Florio.

At the Sebring 12-hour Race, Holbert and Penske took the Sports Class and Index of Performance, but four Ferraris finished in front of them. On the Targa Florio, Dan Gurney and Jo Bonnier took second place behind the Ferrari of Wolfgang von Trips. Stirling Moss and Graham Hill have been called the moral winners of the event in their Camoradi-entered RS60 but, after leading, just five miles from the end, the differential failed -

the World Sports Car Championship, behind Ferrari and Maserati.

Class wins were still coming thick and fast for Porsche but, in 1962, there was nothing better than one second place (taken by Bob Holbert at Nassau), while third place was achieved on six occasions. An outright win in the Sports Car Races remained elusive.

In 1963, however, Jo Bonnier and Carlo Mario Abate won the Targa Florio. Driving an eight-cylinder version of the RS61 coupé, the winning average speed was 64.94mph, slightly quicker than the Ferraris that had won the classic event in the previous two years.

At Le Mans, four Porsches were entered, and all were works supported. There were two 718/8 models (one a coupé and the other an open car), powered by the Grand Prix-inspired eight-cylinder 2 litre engines. As it happened, the Spyder of Barth/Linge was the only Porsche finisher, coming in eighth and winning its Class, despite having lost a wheel at one stage. The other cars were the new 2000GS/GT machines.

The Abarth-Carrera was doing well in its series, but even including the smaller Sports Car Races, the Targa Florio was to remain the only outright victory in 1963. The Spyders were outdated now, but soon a change in direction provided Porsche with the winner's laurels once again.

An era had passed on something of a low note, but as Helmut

Dan Gurney on the 1962 Targa Florio driving a 718 W-RS Spyder.

unfortunately, moral winners don't get to hold the trophy.

The third round in the Championship was at the Nürburgring, but it was a poor showing for the Stuttgart marque. Le Mans was next, and the RS61 Spyder of Gregory and Holbert was the top Porsche, finishing in fifth place overall and first in the two litre Class. Not far behind in seventh was the RS61 coupé of Barth and Herrmann, while Linge and Ben Pol took tenth in their 695GS Abarth-Carrera. The Veuillet-entered 695GS of Buchet/P. Monneret retired one hour from the end, as did the Bonnier/Gurney RS61 coupé. Both cars went out with engine trouble.

Pescara was the final round, but the best Porsche could manage was second place. This was enough, however, to secure the third slot in

Jo Bonnier with the RS61 coupé that he took to victory on the 1963 Targa Florio.

Chassis Numbers

Chassis numbers for the cars covered in this chapter are listed below:

Sports Racing Cars -

550A Spyder	550A0101 to 550A0144
718 RSK	718001 to 718034
RS61 & 718/8	718044 to 718047
RS60	718051 to 718064
RS61	718065 to 718078

Formula Racing Cars -

F2 Type 718/2	718201 to 718205
F2 Type 787	78701 to 78702
F1 Type 804	80401 to 80404

Bott pointed out: "In those days, Spyders and road cars were not so far apart." Porsche insisted on keeping a family relationship between the production and racing cars - even the Grand Prix cars. When one considers this and the fact that the marque's competition, more often than not with far larger engines, was using some very specialised machinery, Porsche's results were all the more commendable.

7

THE 356C
- LAST OF THE LINE

Introduced in July 1963, the 356C was essentially a stopgap model until the new 911 had become established. More refined than its predecessors, the body was very much the same as that seen on the 356B and was offered in coupé and cabriolet form, with the option of a detachable steel hardtop for the latter. There were also better seats and armrests on the doors, but the main changes were mechanical.

New engines developed under Hans Mezger made their debut; the 1600C carried the 75bhp 616/15 power-unit, while the 1600SC had the 95bhp 616/16. All-round disc brakes supplied by Ate (under Dunlop licence) were standard across the range, but there was still a drum mounted on the rear disc for the handbrake. The gearbox housing had been modified, along with the rear suspension, although the transverse leaf spring (as fitted to the 356B Super 90 model) was now made into a special order item.

Denis Jenkinson of *MotorSport* was one of the first people to try the new car: "Several modifications have been made to the current Porsche range and the type is now designated the 356C. The 60bhp model is dropped leaving the 1600C which has 75bhp with improved torque and the 1600SC which has 95bhp at 5800rpm against 90bhp

Publicity shot of the 356C cabriolet, available with 1600C or 1600SC engines.

The 356C coupé was outwardly much the same as the 356B, but there were a number of improvements under the skin. New style wheels (with flat hub caps) were a feature of the latest model.

at 5000rpm of the old Super 90 model. Disc brakes are now standard equipment on all wheels. I was able to drive one of the latest models, and it was soon apparent that Porsche engineers read magazine road-test reports for the heater knob has been replaced by a lever and the awkwardly placed light switch has been moved so that the driver does not have to reach through the steering wheel to operate it. Some suspension modifications have been made including a stiffer roll bar and softer rear springs, but my test drive was too short to detect any noticeable changes."

In January 1965, *Sporting Motorist* tested a 1600SC coupé. They noted: "The Porsche has always been a fiercely individualistic motor car and even after all these years it remains so. Smoother, quieter and more sophisticated than it used to be, it still remains very much a driver's car, with that indefinable ability to respond to the judgement and skill of the man at the wheel. It has its shortcomings, but it is a remarkable tribute to the original design of the car that so much of it is still so good." They clocked a 0-60mph time of 11.1 seconds, and a top speed of 114mph. These figures were mirrored almost exactly by a number of other magazines, so can be deemed fairly accurate.

The price of the 1600SC coupé in the UK at that time was £2278 (including Purchase Tax). Standard colours included Light Ivory, Ruby Red, Signal Red, Slate Grey, Champagne Yellow, Sky Blue and Irish Green, while Black, Togo Brown, Bali Blue and Dolphin Grey could be ordered at extra cost.

In America, by far the most important market for Porsche, the 356C was priced at $4195 for the 1600C coupé, or $4753 for the SC. The cabriolet was priced at $4564 and $5096 for the C and SC versions respectively. The optional

The detachable steel hardtop in place on a 356C cabriolet. Note the new badge at the rear.

Below - Interior shot of a 356C cabriolet. The dashboard was still purely functional, but the Porsche was very comfortable for long-distance journeys.

hardtop would have added around $175. Other major options included chrome-plated wheels ($79), white-wall tyres ($29), an electrically-operated sunroof ($312), leather trim for the coupé ($222) and an AM/FM radio at $253.

The Carrera 2, announced in 1961, was retained in the 356C

Detail of the new Ate disc brakes. This is the rear wheel with its integral handbrake drum.

Below - More luggage space had been afforded through the T-6 body modifications, so naturally the 356C inherited them. Baggage could also be put on the rear seats of course.

range. A British magazine tried a 1964 356C Carrera 2000GS and recorded a 126mph top speed with a 0-60 time of just 9.2 seconds. As we have mentioned earlier, the German DIN power measurement is always on the low side for British and American tests and 152bhp SAE was recorded on the rolling road in the UK.

The Carrera 2 continued into 1965, finally disappearing with the rest of the 356 range. In the meantime, it had gained disc brakes along with the other models when the 356C was introduced. Just 126 356C Carrera 2s were produced (5 of which were right-hand drive) so, today, this was a very rare and desirable motor car, although with original prices starting at $7585 it is perhaps not surprising that so few were built.

Motorsport News

As the 356 grew older, its competition exploits tended to give way to the more specialised racing cars. However, there were still a number of notable achievements. Walter and Lier won the 1963 Geneva Rally outright and, in 1964, the Klass/Wencher pairing won the GT Class of the Monte Carlo Rally. Porsche recorded a Class victory on the Tulip Rally, and J. Rey won a Coupé des Alpes and also the GT Class in the Alpine Rally.

Still in 1964, Bruce Jennings won the title of SCCA Class C (Production) Champion in his Carrera. Fellow American Dick Smith re-

peated this success by taking the same accolade two years later in a similar machine.

Competitors

It is hard to find a direct competitor for the Porsche 356, as few sports cars offered such performance from a small engine and even fewer had their power-units in the back. It is perhaps easier to look at what some of the established sports car

manufacturers were building at the time, and make some suitable comparisons.

German sports cars were few and far between. BMW had the 507 from 1956, but it proved too expensive (even by Porsche standards) to find its deserved place on the best-sellers list. Auto Union sold the 1000SP (based on a DKW chassis) from 1958 to 1965 but, in all this time, less than 7000 were sold. The

Robert Buchet in a works' Carrera battling through the snow on the 1964 Monte Carlo Rally.

Mercedes-Benz 190SL was perhaps the Porsche's closest competitor, with a top speed of just over 100mph and a 0-60 time of 13.3 seconds - nearly 26,000 were sold from 1954 to 1963.

In the same price range, Italy had the delightful Alfa Romeo Giulietta, which was very quick and handled superbly. Like the Porsche, the Giulietta came with a number of body and engine options. Lancia were fielding the technically-brilliant Aurelia, but these were quite costly in export markets.

The masters of the small sports car at the time were the British, with the likes of Triumph, MG, Austin-Healey and, later, Sunbeam and Lotus. With a Triumph TR3 at about half the price of the cheapest Porsche in the UK (or 20 per cent cheaper in America), it was easy to see why the mass-produced British cars were so popular. Even specialist manufacturers like Jaguar could undercut the 356 on the home market, or at least equal it in America and the Coventry cars were much faster of course.

America was slow to enter the sports car field. The Chevrolet Corvette was around the same price; one was tested alongside the Convertible D in 1959 and, although the 'Vette outperformed the German car comfortably, it was declared a draw by the magazine's panel. The Ford Thunderbird, introduced in 1955, was cheaper than both the Porsche and the Corvette. It could also perform well thanks to its mighty engine, and over 50,000 units were sold in just two years.

As can be seen, it certainly wasn't the price that sold the little Porsche. The 356 obviously appealed to those who wanted to be different and to those who appreciated the German engineering and quality control.

Porsche turnover in 1965 amounted to around 200,000,000DM, so the company must have been doing something right! Even Graham Hill, one of the finest Grand Prix drivers of all time, was moved enough to say "Hmmm, bloody good car" following a fast drive. However, by now the 356's long-awaited replacement had established itself in the market.

Death of the 356

The basic layout of four air-cooled

A 356C 1600SC coupé and its ultimate replacement, the 911. These pictures date from late 1964, a time when the two models would have been built and sold alongside each other.

A 356C 1600SC coupé and its replacement pictured from the rear. The family resemblance between 356 and 911 is very obvious.

What should have been the very last 356, then the Dutch police ordered another ten. Anyway, officially, this was the final one, and the end of an era.

356C Chassis Numbers

As with the 356B, the Karmann-bodied coupés have been separated from the Reutter-bodied cars. Officially, Karmann stopped body production on 21 January 1965 and Reutter (who were taken over by Porsche in March 1964) stopped on 28 April 1965. Porsche thought that a white cabriolet completed in September was going to be the last car, and indeed it was officially, but then the Dutch police placed a special order for ten vehicles in 1966 - they were initiated in March.

1963 coupé	126001 to 128104
1963 Karmann coupé	215001 to 216738
1963 cabriolet	159001 to 159832
1964 coupé	128105 to 131927
1964 Karmann coupé	216739 to 221482
1964 cabriolet	159833 to 161577
1965 coupé	131928 to 131930
1965 Karmann coupé	221483 to 222579
1965 cabriolet	161578 to 162155
1966 cabriolet	162156 to 162165

Exchange chassis supplied from 1953 to 1965 (all models) - 5601 to 5624/12201 to 12376/13001 to 13414

cylinders, horizontally opposed in pairs, remained unchanged throughout the seventeen year lifespan of the 356 and the body had changed little. However, throughout the whole life of the car features tested in the field of motorsport were added. As you will have read in the previous chapters, the 356 also provided the basis for a number of highly-successful sports racers and, with the 911, was developed into one of the most desirable road cars ever built.

Denis Jenkinson, who used to entertain thousands of enthusiasts when covering the European scene for *MotorSport* magazine, once wrote: "It was not so much a car that was ahead of its time as a car of its time. It set the postwar standards for sports and GT cars, leading the field for a long time, and while many people tried to follow Professor Porsche's original conception, few succeeded ..."

But it was Mike McCarthy of *Classic & Sportscar* who summed up the 356 perfectly: "The number '356' is hardly memorable. It doesn't roll off the tongue, it doesn't sound poetic, it could be the most anonymous number you could think of between 1 and 1000. Yet to motoring enthusiasts generally, and Porscheophiles in particular, those three digits have a very special significance. They were applied to one of the greatest sports cars the world has ever seen."

PORSCHE 356

8

A NEW GENERATION

Despite the continuing demand for the 356, it was obvious that the model was not going to last forever, and, in the late-fifties, Porsche started to prepare for its ultimate replacement. Ferry Porsche wanted the new car to be slightly bigger and a true 2+2. The Type 695 project began in 1959. Built on the same 94.5 inch wheelbase as the Type 530 (four-seater 356) prototype, it was first given the internal T-7 designation, implying that it was initially considered as little more than a 356 update.

However, with the flat-four get-ting close to the end of its develop-ment, it was also necessary to look at a new power-unit. The flat-four was powerful enough in Carrera guise, but these units were expen-sive to build so, in 1961, design work on a new power-unit was ini-tiated.

The 911 and 912

The six-cylinder engine was ready for testing in the early part of 1962 but, by this time, the four-seater idea had again been rejected. Although the Type 695 never did see the light of day, many of its

The Type 695 prototype photographed in 1961. It was given the T-7 designation, implying that it was the next in the Porsche 356 series of bodies - could this have been the 356D?

The 901 with its designer Butzi Porsche (standing on the right) in 1963. Butzi Porsche has never been fully appreciated as one of the world's best car designers.

lines were carried through to give the now legendary shape of the 911.

The new model's coupé body was styled by Butzi Porsche and given the design number 901. Butzi (actually Ferdinand Alexander) was the oldest of Ferry Porsche's sons, being born in 1935. He had joined Porsche's Styling Department in 1957, but this was not just a case of providing jobs for the family, Butzi would go on to be a very accomplished designer. Erwin Komenda did the engineering side of the bodywork.

As the months passed, the Type 901 project came ever closer to becoming reality and it was decided that the flat-eight Grand Prix engine would form the basis for the

new car's power unit. Shortened to a six-cylinder layout, and using just one overhead-camshaft per bank instead of two, the 130bhp two litre engine was also given the Type 901 designation - it was developed by Hans Tomola.

The Porsche 901, whilst retaining many of the features of its predecessor, was a completely new car. Although the rear-mounted air-cooled boxer engine layout was kept, along with the famous Porsche baulk-ring gearbox and all-round independent suspension, it was a larger car.

The 901 was first seen at the Frankfurt Show in 1963, but the production cars wouldn't roll off the line at Zuffenhausen until the following year. *MotorSport* reported

on the 901 in October: "The car itself remains unmistakably a Porsche in appearance except for its longer wheelbase and different front and rear end styling."

It was not long, however, before the 901 designation was altered to 911: Peugeot had complained about Porsche encroaching on "their" numbering system (*ie* having a zero in the middle of a three-figure model identifying number). In fact, the Peugeot numbering system was only registered in France, but this was a big sales outlet for Porsche so, to save marketing problems later, 901 was changed to 911 before the car went on sale.

The 911 was made available to the public at 21,900DM following a

The Porsche 912 - basically a 911 body powered by the 356 engine.

Below - Interior of the 912.

successful 1964 Frankfurt Show then, in May 1965, Porsche introduced the 912. The body, suspension and braking system were identical to the six-cylinder 911, but the 912 was far closer to the 356 in that it used the Super 90 (616/16) power-unit. The 911 was produced alongside the 356 in the latter's final years.

The 911 was introduced to the American public at Albany, California, in July 1965. The 912 was announced two months later, just as the 356 series officially ran out. The American market remained the most important for Porsche and its pricing policy there was interesting. In its final year, an SC coupé would have cost $4577 in basic form, while the 911 was $6490. The 912, however, was just $4690 - about the same as the earlier model.

Initially two versions of the 912 were on offer: the 912/4 with four-speed transmission and the 912/5 with a five-speed 'box. Whereas the 911 had five gauges on the wood-trimmed fascia, the 912 only had three and no wood trim. Capable of around 115mph, 0-60 came up in a fraction under twelve seconds - about the same as the 356C 1600SC coupé.

6472 Type 912 Porsches were built during 1965, followed by 8700 in 1966. For the 1967 model year, a four-speed manual 'box was the only transmission available on the 912. During the year, a total of 3239 912s were built and, for 1968,

they came with the five-speed option again. The most important change, though, was the availability of the Targa body (announced in September 1965, but not sold until the following year) and listed for both the 911 and 912.

During 1969, the 912 coupé was $5095, while the 912 Targa was $5615. During 1968 and 1969, a total of 11,921 912s were built, but this was to be the last year for the 912 as it made way for the mid-engined 914.

On the 1965 Monte Carlo Rally, special stages were used for the

first time. Porsche entered one of their sports models (the 904), which finished an incredible second in the hands of Eugen Bohringer and Rolf Wütherich. They also entered a 911 crewed by Herbert Linge and Peter Falk, it finished fifth and took a two litre Class win in the process. Wütherich was best-known as James Dean's old racing mechanic and was actually Dean's passenger on the day of his fatal crash. Eugen Bohringer was an ex-Mercedes-Benz works driver. He had nine international rally successes with Benz and was European Cham-

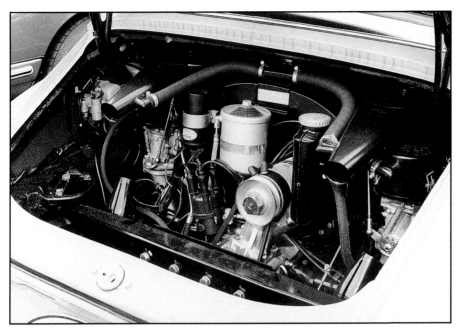

The old Type 616/16 (Super 90) engine in place in the 912.

Below - The Targa body was announced in 1965 for both the 911 and 912 models, but it would be well over a decade before Porsche released a convertible in the 911 range.

in 1970. Waldegard also won the Swedish Rally three years in succession from 1968 onwards for Porsche.

S. Zasada and E. Zasada won the 1967 Polish Rally in a 912; they won again two years later in a

pion Rally Driver in 1962, but the 1965 result, in what was supposed to be an unsuitable car, was outstanding.

In the 1967 Monte Carlo Rally,

Vic Elford took third place in a 911S. The following year he would win the event, with Bjorn Waldegard proving it was no fluke for the Stuttgart concern in 1969 and again

911S. The 911 and its smaller-engined sister were already proving their worth in competition and the 911 would go on to far greater things. Approximately 50,979 911

Porsches were produced from 1965 to 1969 although, during the last of these years, a second generation 911 had been launched. During the same period 30,332 912s had been built.

Competition Cars - the 904

Ferry Porsche gave the go-ahead for a new car at the end of 1962. To comply with the FIA regulations for the Grand Touring Championship at least 100 examples would have to be built, thus ruling out labour-intensive spaceframes and handmade bodies.

"The new Porsche is designated the Type 904, not to be confused with Type 901 which is the touring six-cylinder that appeared recently at all the Motor Shows. The new 904 is a complete break from Porsche tradition in its construction, for it has a chassis frame comprised of two deep-section box members, suitably cross-braced, whereas previous Porsche coupés

Edgar Barth and Herbert Linge testing the 904 at Solitude in November 1963. Barth dominated the hillclimb season in 1963 (and again in 1964) with the new car. Note the early rear air intake.

have been of monocoque construction, made from thin sheet steel or sheet aluminium. The 904 chassis has double wishbone and coil-spring front suspension, rack-and-pinion steering, double-wishbone and coil-spring rear suspension, all of which is directly descended from the Grand Prix Porsche eight-cylinders. The air-cooled two litre Carrera four-cylinder engine is mounted ahead of the rear axle and

Left - A Porsche 911 (background) about to embark on the 1965 Monte Carlo Rally; it finished fifth. In the foreground is the 904GTS also driven on the event, which took second place.

904 body production at Heinkel. It was such a light body that just two people could lift it.

drives to a five-speed Porsche gearbox and the drive is taken to the independently-sprung rear wheels through one-piece driveshafts having very clever inboard universal joints that not only swivel in all planes, but also extend in and out on short links, giving friction-free movement to the rear end. These new universal joints achieve by mechanical means exactly the same effect as Lotus arrive at with the rubber-ring 'doughnut' universal joints used on their racing cars." - *MotorSport* 1964.

The lightweight glassfibre body (designed by Butzi Porsche) was bonded to the chassis for extra strength. Porsche had no real experience of working in glassfibre, so contracted out the work to Heinkel Flugzeubau - a company better-known for bombers and bubble cars rather than exotic bodyshells. Glassfibre was chosen for speed of production - four to five cars a day had to be built in order for the model to qualify in time for the 1964 season.

The intention was to build 100 examples with the four-cylinder Carrera engine for homologation purposes and then to make a small series as works' cars with six- and eight-cylinder engines. After that, a second series of 100 cars would be built for the 1965 season solely with six-cylinder power-units and with an evolution certificate for GT competitions.

As was the practice at Porsche, the road and race cars remained

The 904 with the air intakes modified to stop the brakes from overheating. This is actually a 904/8 works car.

linked and the 904 used the five-speed gearbox, steering and braking system that would later be employed on the 911 when it entered production. The top speed was approximately 160mph, with a 0-60 time hovering around the 5.5 second mark.

The price for the Carrera GTS - the customer car - was less than 30,000DM, which was quite cheap for a racing machine. Porsche kept

the first ten for themselves, but the vast majority of the remainder were sold within weeks. Records show that 120 were built: 104 cars were made and sold with four-cylinder engines, and of the sixteen 904s retained by the works, ten had six-cylinder engines and six had the eight-cylinder unit.

Its first major race was at Sebring in March 1964 where it ran as a prototype - it was not homolo-

The Type 906 Spyder pictured on 30 September 1965 at Hockenheim. For the 1966 hillclimb season, the record-breaking car was given a coupé body to comply with regulations.

gated until April. The top finisher was ninth overall (and first in Class) for Briggs Cunningham and Lake Underwood. Shortly after, driven by Colin Davis (the son of the famous journalist and racing driver, Sammy) and Antonio Pucci, it won the 1964 Targa Florio; Linge and Balzarini finished second.

Seven 904 models made it to the start line for the 1964 Le Mans 24-hour Race, the 904 being the sole representative of the Stuttgart marque. Two were eight-cylinder 904/8 models contesting the Prototype Class, but these retired (both with clutch trouble). The five other standard 904 GTS models were placed in the GT Class and all finished. The Veuillet-entered car of Buchet and Guy Ligier was the best placed, coming seventh. The other cars recorded eighth, tenth, 11th, and 12th respectively.

The Davis/Mitter pairing took second place in the ugly 904 Spyder prototype on the 1965 Targa Florio, behind Vaccarella's Ferrari. The car was later written off at the Nürburgring. The 1965 Le Mans event was to be the last appearance of the 904s in the French classic. The 904/6 of Linge and Nöcker came fourth overall, powered by the six-cylinder engine that could be seen in the 911 road car. A works-entered four-cylinder 904 GTS finished fifth and took the Index of Efficiency award. The other five 904s failed to complete the course.

The 904 dominated two litre

sports car racing during 1964 and 1965. In terms of overall wins the 904 was not as successful as the previous 718s, but it did set Porsche on the route that led to a decade of competition success.

Car & Driver said "the owner/driver would have to be slightly out of his mind to use it on the highway" but a small number of people did. The fact that the 904 did so well on the Monte Carlo Rally proves beyond any doubt that it was not just a wild racer. Porsche did look at the idea of a luxury 904GTS road car, but a number of problems shelved the idea.

Ferry Porsche had already approved another 100 cars to be built for the 1966 season, but then Ferdinand Piech took over the competition shop. Piech had other ideas: from now on, Porsche's philosophy on racing changed as the company moved further and further away from their road car models. The

904 was to be the last competition model in which the Fuhrmann four-cam Carrera engine was used.

The 906 and 910

Ferdinand Piech, Ferry Porsche's nephew, took over the Research & Development department from Hans Tomola in 1965, having joined the company two years earlier. He was heading towards his thirtieth birthday at the time and was fiercely ambitious. Piech was not concerned that the cars manufactured by the factory for racing bore little or no resemblance to the contemporary production models. With the competition side now coming under the R & D banner, this was his chance to shine.

A spaceframe-based Spyder was built using the Grand Prix Type 771 eight-cylinder engine developing 240bhp. Making its debut at Ollon-Villars hillclimb on 29 August 1965, this was the first

The Scuderia Filipinetti 906 Carrera 6 on the 1966 Targa Florio. The pairing of Willy Mairese and Herbert Müller took the car to a superb victory.

design under Piech and, in the following year, it was rebuilt as a coupé to comply with new rules. Gerhard Mitter took five straight wins and the year's Championship title.

In the meantime, at Hockenheim at the end of the 1965 season, Huschke von Hanstein took the 906 Spyder to new World Records for the 500 metre and quarter-mile distances, the car covering the latter from standstill in 11.89 seconds, which was extremely impressive for the time. He later also took the 1000 metre Record at 22.21 seconds. This car formed the basis for the next works' racer.

The 906 or "Carrera 6" (not to be confused with the ten 904s built with six-cylinder 911-based engines, known internally as the Type 906), was produced to keep the Stuttgart firm competitive against the two litre Ferraris. Powered by a 210bhp six- or 260bhp eight-cylinder engine, it was the first in a long

and victorious line of racing cars designed by the team that was responsible for all the other competition vehicles up to and including the 917.

The first car, ready in January 1966, featured a tubular spaceframe chassis as, to comply with the homologation regulations, only fifty needed to be produced and, on such a small run, it was as cheap to build a spaceframe for each car as to tool-up for a pressed steel chassis. However, the model used a number of 904 components (Ferry Porsche had already bought a great deal of them ready to build the proposed second run of 904 models and there was no way he was going to let them go to waste).

Homologated in May 1966, the 906 made its debut at Le Mans with both long- and short-tail models on show. Finishing fourth, fifth, sixth and seventh overall, it is interesting to note that the 911 (also making its debut at Le Mans in this

year) entered by Jacques Dewez, managed 14th overall at an average of 98.94mph.

The 906 completed the transition of Porsche's motorsport philosophy from road/race cars to pure racers. Whereas the 904 could be driven on normal roads, as Bohringer had proved in the Monte Carlo Rally and Stoop had proved in the streets of the UK, with the 906 it was almost impossible.

The next cars were even further removed from road cars. Ferdinand Piech intended the 910 to take the two litre crown in the 1967 World Championship for Makes - in the end, it nearly got the overall title. Among numerous outstanding victories, Porsche won the Targa Florio in 1966, 1967, 1968, 1969 and 1970 (all with different drivers) and again in 1973. Ernst Fuhrmann returned to Porsche from the Goetze piston ring company in 1972, taking the place of Piech.

911 & 912 Chassis Numbers

The chassis batch numbers of the cars mentioned in this chapter are noted below -

Road Cars -

911	From 300001 onwards
912 coupé	350001 to 355601
	12820001 to 12820427
	12900001 to 12900428
912 K-coupé	450001 to 463204
	12800001 to 12805598
	129020001 to 129023450
912 Targa	550001 to 550544
	12870001 to 12871217
	129010001 to 129010801

Racing Cars -

904/6 and 904/8	904001 to 904006
904 GTS	904007 to 904106
906	906001 to 906003
	906007 to 906010
	906101 to 906158
910 coupé	910001 to 910028
910 spyder	910030 to 910034

It's interesting to note, given the close bond between race and road cars during the 356 era, that Fuhrmann considered the current breed of racing cars (*ie* the all-conquering 917s that followed the 910 and 907) were too far removed from the road cars to be of any real use in marketing. It will be remembered that not long after his new appointment, a whole range of sporting machines stemmed from the 911 and, once again, the Porsche road and racing cars were unequivocally linked.

First spotted late in 1994, the Porsche 968 Boxster may be bigger than a 911, but it is the spiritual successor to the 550 Spyder. In many ways it resembles that car in concept, layout and looks, but this new machine has 240bhp. Expected to go on sale from mid-1996, it is interesting to ponder on whether this might be considered a racing car for the road, which is what I'm sure Ferry Porsche would like to think.

PORSCHE

356

9

BUYING AND RESTORATION

This chapter contains advice on the purchase, maintenance and running of Porsche 356 models.

Body

The key to buying a good 356 is the body - rust is the biggest problem any owner has to face and there is the potential for lots of it. The important thing to watch for (often easier said than done) is the car that has been quickly bodged and resprayed for a fast sale in the days of over-inflated prices. Anyway, here are a few pointers to help steer the potential buyer in the right direction.

The nose is quite susceptible to damage, especially on the earlier cars where the bumpers often do little or nothing to protect the body. Many owners also chose to run their vehicles without bumpers at all, so accident repairs should be looked at carefully. All panels should be free of ripples and fit very

Vulnerable nose area, headlight apertures, wheel well and battery carrier are all very prone to rust. (Courtesy Roger Bray Restorations).

The areas where the front wings join the body at the doors and the bottom hinge are common rust traps. (Courtesy Roger Bray Restorations).

Below - The area around what, on any other car, would be the door sills, should be checked very carefully. (Courtesy Roger Bray Restorations).

well for a car of this era, with neat consistent shut lines of around 3.5mm width.

Headlight apertures and the vent holes in the front wings are favourite places for rust to start and, although most 356 panels are available now (at least the classic car "boom" did something good for enthusiasts - it wasn't that long ago when many panels were unobtainable), it should be borne in mind that parts are expensive.

Doors tend to rot in all the usual places, especially along the bottoms due to blocked drainage holes, but look carefully at the bottom hinge area and where the wings join the body at the doors - common rust areas. Look, too, about halfway up the front wings where the body joins the chassis: a gap here filled with underseal tends to breed moisture, and therefore rust, in the long-term. There is also a water trap where the wing turns over onto the chassis.

Although the underbody is quite streamlined, rust attacks along the seams and is often hidden by underseal. The jacking points are very prone to deterioration and should be inspected carefully. This area often rots, allowing the floor to rust itself free of the inner and outer side (longitudinal) members, which themselves have a habit of rusting badly - bad news considering that a lot of the body's strength comes from these "sills."

The front and rear closing panels should also be looked at, along

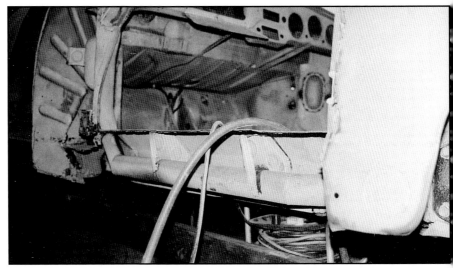

with the footwells, especially where the A-bracket of the front suspension joins the floor. The latter area is very difficult to replace, and is sometimes cracked through pressure from the suspension as well as being rusty.

The centre tunnel, which carries a number of wires and pipes, has been known to come adrift from the floor at each end, and the

luggage compartment has a habit of filling up with water if a car has been left standing outside. This leads to the spare wheel well rotting through and the battery carrier also, which has the additional problem of battery acid to contend with.

As open cars are the most desirable and therefore the most expensive to buy, it's ironic that they

The result of rain entering an open car often is serious corrosion like this. (Courtesy Roger Bray Restorations).

New panels will almost certainly be needed in any restoration project. Reproduction items are available, but many opt for the 'real' thing from Porsche to avoid problems of fit. (Courtesy Roger Bray Restorations).

glassfibre. In America especially, some owners, not being able to source the correct part - as they were often unavailable at the time - fitted glassfibre panels designed for replica 356s (the subject of the next chapter). Some were very good, being moulded off original panels, others less so.

The important thing to remember is that the 356, like most of its contemporaries, is known for its rust problems. In the 1970s, when these cars were very cheap, many fell into the wrong hands and were run into the ground, then later "restored" poorly and resold. A professional quality body restoration could take as long as 400 hours if the experience of the firm owned by Austrian, Richard Kaan, is anything to go by.

The moral of this story is that it is better to buy an original car as a basket-case and spend the money on a proper restoration by a specialist (even Porsche themselves can do this, or the Porsche Club can recommend a number of people) or buy a well-restored machine from a reputable dealer. Cars priced in the mid-range rarely provide the buyer with a bargain: with the non-Carrera cars, the real value of the machine lies in the body condition.

A final note: do not rely purely on a photographic record as a basis for buying a car - it might not be of the car you are buying!

Engine

There is nothing really special to

should be the most susceptible to rust - buyer beware. The front and rear floorpan joints are more at risk on these models, as are the more obvious areas such as inner door panels and pillars due to their exposure. A good tip is to lift a car at each corner to see if the shut lines alter.

If the coupé is fitted with an electric sunroof (available from September 1961), check its operation, as restoring this item is very difficult, often testing even the most experienced mechanics.

One other item which a potential buyer may, or may not, come across is reproduction panels in

look out for on the standard 356 cars, just the usual rumblings, blue smoke, and so on. Fortunately, the mechanical components of the Porsche 356 are known for their robustness but, naturally, a deep rumbling noise could well mean a bottom-end rebuild which, although not extortionate, will knock a serious dent in the average buyers' budget (perhaps as much as $4500/£3000 at the time of writing).

Oil leaks from the bell housing should be investigated and minor leaks are commonly found around the rocker boxes, oil cooler and the seal on the gear selector. In an ideal world there should be no leaks at all, but start to become suspicious if the engine has recently been steam cleaned and looks unnaturally clean in relation to the condition of the rest of the car.

A steady warm oil pressure should be recorded and the tickover should be quiet with no lumpiness once warm. Above all, the engine should provide smooth and strong performance. Watch out for cars that have been fitted with non-original parts sourced from the Beetle, as the whole car may have been maintained "on the cheap."

The good news is that engine parts are readily available from a number of specialists around the world and at least 100,000 miles should be possible before an engine rebuild, provided regular oil and filter changes are carried out.

Carrera four-cam engines are another matter and should only be tackled by specialists because of their great complexity and current value. With the Carrera models, it's the engine rather than the body in which the true value of the car lies.

Gearbox

The gearchange should be light and precise and the gearbox is well-known for its strength. Whilst driving the car, the potential buyer should check for the usual items such as worn synchromesh or the whining of bearings: there should be no noise or excessive play in the gearlever. Gearbox rebuilds are, fortunately, not particularly expensive and parts are readily available.

Suspension

Whilst test driving, listen for the usual clonks found on ill-maintained cars, and pay particular attention to the link pins in the front suspension. Jacking the vehicle up at the front until the wheel is clear of the ground is a good way of finding play in the suspension and steering. After making sure the car is safe (through the use of axle stands), rock the road wheel at the top and bottom - clunking noises will reveal worn link pins, which should either be adjusted or replaced if in poor condition. Naturally, both sides of the car should be inspected.

Suspension mountings should be checked for corrosion, along with the bump stops and trailing arm mounts at the back. The area around the front anti-roll bar should also be inspected.

Steering

Steering is by worm and peg, and play in the steering can be checked very easily. Inside the luggage compartment is a small inspection hatch and, by having someone gently rock the steering wheel from side to side, excessive play in the assembly can quickly be spotted.

While one of the front wheels is up in the air (when checking the suspension) rock the road wheel with your hands at the quarter-to-three position. Clunking noises here will show play in the steering (the wheels should be pointing straight ahead when carrying out this check).

The test drive should show the car to be tight in all respects, with the controls giving precise movements. If not, again, all steering and suspension parts are readily available from a vast number of specialists, although shopping around does pay - some parts can

The finished result of a beautiful restoration. This was actually the first cabriolet imported into Britain which was displayed at the 1951 Earls Court Show.

be a little expensive.

Braking system
Drum brakes were fitted to earlier cars, whilst discs all-round were a feature on the later models (the 356Cs). The steel drum liner should be inspected if a car has been in storage for a long time, as it has been known for the surface to deteriorate badly. If a buyer is thinking of converting a left-hand drive car to right-hand drive, pedal boxes are one of the few items that are hard to come by for the 356.

Wheels & tyres
Wheels are available if the originals are too bad to use (rust often takes hold in the join between the rim and centre plate) and various modern 165 x 15 radial tyres can be used (radials were actually fitted as standard from the 356B). Early cars used either a 3 or 3.25in x 16in rim while, from the 356A onwards, a 4.5in x 15in version was specified.

Remember of course that abnormal wear on the tyres can tell you a lot about the condition of the mechanical components and/or the chassis.

Trim
Although there is now very little excuse for not having a car in its original specification, this was not always the case and buyers should be familiar with the model they are going to look at before setting off. A car that is scruffy but complete

and correct is far better than one that looks good, but has been trimmed with a complete disregard for originality.

There is nothing inherently bad about a car with non-original specification, if that's what you choose (after all, the whole of the custom movement can't be wrong) but, remember, if you want to dispose of the car later, you may have trouble selling it to a dealer or collector. In addition, parts for the pre-A models are hard to come by and most of them are expensive, supposing of course that the buyer would like an original-looking vehicle.

The usual checks on the general condition of the interior and its fittings (such as window winders) should be carried out, but particular attention should be paid to the front seat backrests. These tend to be a source of irritation as their screws work loose, causing the metal which attaches the backrest to the reclining mechanism to flex and eventually sheer - when this happens, the seat literally falls apart. Remember, the condition of the driver's seat and pedal rubbers is often a good guide to the true mileage of a vehicle.

It's a good idea to check the window sealing rubbers, as perished rubber will undoubtedly have let water into the car, thus setting off rust problems. Hoods are now available as reproduction items, as indeed are most components that go towards finishing off a car. The Porsche spares back-up is now very

good in Europe, America and Japan.

Electrics
Almost all 356s had 6v electrical systems (*à la* Volkswagen Beetle), although the last few to be produced were equipped with a 12v system. Over the years many owners have updatedtheir cars to 12v electrics and this should not be regarded as a bad thing, unless the buyer is looking for a show car - after all, 12v systems allow for better headlight illumination and cold weather reliability. Most electrical parts have been reproduced now, including lights and their lenses.

Fuel system
Solex carburettors were used throughout production, except for the rather specialised Carrera models. Some of the Carreras used Weber units, but we have deliberately left these desirable cars out of this buyers guide - they should only be bought by really experienced Porsche people as their rarity and value makes them too risky for the average enthusiast to buy. If you see one and want one, contact the Porsche Club and ask for advice first.

Running costs
Although running a 356 will never be cheap, the model does at least offer a decided advantage over the 911 once it has been made good. The emphasis here is on *once* it has been made good, as the 356 is like

most classic cars - it is easier and cheaper to maintain a really good car than carry out a running restoration whilst using the vehicle.

Of course, if the buyer is a skilled amateur mechanic or is not too worried about originality, a 356 can be run on a shoestring (work on the body, however, is quite a specialised job and should not be tackled by anyone with a less than professional approach). It should be said though, if the potential buyer is not worried about keeping the car original and in perfect condition, it might be better to buy a replica and save on a lot of the heartache and expense.

Regular servicing is the key to a happy relationship between car and owner and, in this respect, it should be borne in mind that the later the car the more complicated it will be. However, apart from the Carrera models, normal routine maintenance should not be beyond the scope of the capable enthusiast with the right tools and a proper workshop manual.

Which one?

The pre-A and 356A models are without doubt the cars for the Porsche purist. These are the earliest examples of the breed, and perhaps the prettiest, but not the most practical. The 356C is definitely the more refined car and could probably be put to everyday use quite happily with regular servicing - a more powerful range of engines, disc brakes and a better environment within the cabin all add to its appeal.

However, it is the 356B that will probably catch the eye of most enthusiasts, as it is halfway between the two. It is equally as enjoyable to drive over long distances and should be easier to find nowadays as most of the early cars worth saving have been found. Also there were roughly twice as many 356Bs built as 356Cs.

Whether to go for a coupé or cabriolet is of course a matter of personal taste and depends a lot on what use the car is to be put to. As an all year round everyday vehicle it would probably be sensible to run a coupé. For fair weather use and those with slightly bigger budgets, a convertible will be the 356 of choice. Whatever your choice, a good car should prove to be a sound investment in relation to the alternative of buying a modern car and suffering its depreciation in value.

The most important thing to bear in mind when contemplating buying a 356 is that restoration work is quite specialised and often far from cheap. What might seem a bargain on the face of it may well end up costing you far more than buying a good restored example in the first place. Get advice from the Porsche Club in your country - the relatively small cost of an expert inspection could save you a fortune!

PORSCHE 356

10

REPLICAS

This chapter is, hopefully, a comprehensive guide to the 356 replicas and kit cars available (past and present) from all over the world. Some are still available and some are better than others, but they all have one thing in common - the look of a classic Porsche. They are presented here in alphabetical order.

Apal

Automobiles Apal started building their Speedster replicas in 1981 having obtained a licence to build the Intermeccanica in Belgium. The Belgian company were always happy to supply the car in kit form or as a turnkey model.

The Apal continues to be built to this day in Blegny, its 1.6 litre 50bhp VW motor powering it to 97mph.

The Apal is perhaps one of the more famous replicas, but it should be noted that the company also produced a number of Porsche-Abarth lookalikes based on the VW Beetle, and later around the 356 Super 90 engine itself. Around 150 of these coupés were built from 1961 to 1965.

Beck Development

This California-based company market an impressive fibreglass replica of the 550 Spyder known as the "Beck Spyder" (or "Vintage 550 Spyder"). Using a Volkswagen Beetle or Porsche 356/912 air-cooled power-unit, outputs can vary from 34bhp to well over 100bhp. Having originated from Brazil, the car is available from the American enthusiast and ex-racing driver, Chuck Beck, in kit form, although

Vintage 550 Spyder
Driver: Chuck Beck

The Beck Development "Vintage 550 Spyder" seen here being driven by Charles Beck.

The Chesil Speedster, based on a shortened VW floorpan.

a number of fully-built machines were supplied in the past.

Everything is available to make the Beck Spyder "as near-perfect a replica as you're likely to find." About 800 Beck Spyders (kits and fully-built) have been sold to date.

Beck was also responsible for a 904 GTS replica and, more recently, an impressive 356 Speedster. The Speedster could be supplied with a 300bhp turbocharged VW power-unit, although 120bhp was the norm. Sadly, neither are produced any more.

Chesil Speedster

Since 1991 Peter Bailey has marketed the Street Beetle Company's Speedster from new premises near Bridport in Dorset, England, and has upheld a commitment to quality and authenticity. He added an integral heating system and made further improvements in the comfort and quality of the car which is now known as the Chesil (after a local beach) Speedster.

Based on the 1957 model of the Speedster, the Chesil Speedster has a rigid self-coloured glassfibre bodyshell with its own built-in tubular steel frame which bolts directly onto a shortened VW Beetle floorpan. Chesil offer engine options of 1.6 litre (60bhp), 1.8 litre (90bhp), and 2 litre (110bhp).

As the company's brochure says: "The Chesil Speedster creates an atmosphere for you to settle in and become part of the driv-

ing experience. For a nostalgic feel of the 1950s or the progressive pace of today, the Chesil is a willing partner in your return to pure motoring."

A recent addition to the Chesil range is the company's 550 Spyder replica. It is built at the Dorset works thanks to a special arrangement with Chamonix Industria Comercio Ltda, which formally marketed the Chamonix 550 Spyder in Germany. Available with engines of 1.6 to 2 litres capacity, performance should be excellent.

Classic Motor Carriages

This company produced the Beetle-engined Classic Speedster, a replica of the 356A. Based in Miami in America, at one point the company employed 200 people to manufacture 300 cars per month, either in kit form or as finished vehicles. The interesting thing about this concern is that they offered the Classic Speedster C, which was basically a racing version featuring wider wheels and tyres under larger wheelarches, an American specification rollover bar, and a more powerful engine.

Covin Speedster

Nick Vincent and Tim Cook formed Covin Performance Mouldings in 1983 and quickly established a worldwide reputation for quality.

The Covin Speedster appeared in 1989 as a replica of the 356 Speedster. Based on the Volkswagen Beetle floorpan and running gear the kit was produced in Essex, England.

The Covin concern also produced a Porsche 911 replica, available as either a coupé or cabriolet; there is also the option of an attractive 935-style nose. Now, Grand Performance Cars have taken over the company, but they have continued building the Speedster model.

DJ Sportscars

The makers of the well-known Dax Cobra replica also tried their hand at a Porsche 356. Their advertising from 1984 read: "Subtle and refined in typical German sports car style, our Porsche 356 Speedster Replica is a sincere reproduction of an all-time classic. The beautifully made, double-skinned bodyshell is accurately detailed, has a factory fitted subframe and mates to a shortened VW floorpan."

Dax are still in business today, but the Dax Speedster did not last long, though marketed for a time through Sandwood Automotive of Tamworth, England. The latter would also supply the car in "California Speedster" specification, which basically meant minus any of the detailing.

Envemo Super 90

A Brazilian replica of the 356C in both coupé and cabriolet form, introduced in late-1979. The owner of the company, Luis Fernando Goncalves, is a recognised Porsche enthusiast, having owned a number of interesting examples of the marque. He used a shortened VW Brasilia chassis, with the standard 1.6 litre engine rated at 65bhp and powerful enough to give 97mph (1.8, 1.9 and 2 litre power-units were also available). Because this was a first class replica, they sold, literally, all over the world. For a short time, during the early-1980s, they were even sold through a Porsche dealership in Schorndorf, Germany!

Fiberfab

The American Fiberfab concern was formed in 1965 and produced a number of fibreglass bodies for mounting on the venerable VW Beetle chassis. The first "Aztec" model of 1965 resembled the Porsche 904GTS in profile, although it was never actively marketed as a replica. However, by the late-1980s, the company was concentrating on its 356A Speedster clone and a customised version of the same car known as the "Speedster California."

Flat 4 "Vintage Speedster"

A 356 Speedster replica, beautifully detailed by the Japanese Flat 4 company (a classic Volkswagen specialist) in Tokyo, Japan. Although the car's retrospective looks are obviously of great appeal, it has a twin-carburettor 1584cc engine giving 75bhp. The car comes in authentic period colours such as Black, Ivory, Signal Red or Silver and with interior colour options of Black, Tan or Red; the hood colours are either Black or Tan depending on the coachwork.

GP Spyder

The GP Spyder is manufactured and marketed by GP Projects (or GP Specialist Vehicles) of Middlesex, England, who specialize in the design and building of one-off vehicles. GP is one of the best-known and most respected names in the kit car industry, with nearly three decades of experience behind it.

The Spyder, created by Neville Trickett, is modelled on the sports racing Porsche 718 (or RSK). The glassfibre body is so authentic that it is hardly distinguishable from the real thing.

Production began in 1983 and, by the 1990s, the range included a kit to convert the Spyder into an RS60 model. Various Volkswagen engines, from 1.2 to 2.2 litres could be fitted, the latter giving the lightweight machine an excellent turn of speed. Writing for *Classic & Sportscar*, Mike McCarthy stated: "I picked up the GP Spyder a sceptic - and left it thoroughly impressed, much to my astonishment. It is Fun with a capital F."

Intermecccanica

The Automobili Intermeccanica business could be the subject of a book in itself. Founded in Turin in 1958 by Frank Reisner, the Intermeccanica company produced a selection of sports cars (their most famous being the Italia and the Indra) and a number of prototypes for other companies, including the first Lamborghini. The company was sold in 1976 to Tony Baumgartner, the owner of a Californian VW dealership and, in the following year, work began on the replica Porsche Speedster.

Handbuilt in glassfibre, it is not known quite how many were built - around 650 is one conservative estimate. With its 1640cc 90bhp VW engine the car was ca-

The TPC Motor Company handled the Apal in the UK. Nowadays, the Classic Carriage Company do this from their base not far from the Mallory Park race circuit.

range of kits was available, with VW engine options from 1.2 to 1.6 litres.

By 1991, the car was being marketed as the Chesil Speedster and being produced in Bridport instead of Christchurch. The Chesil Speedster is still in production.

Technic

A shortlived British replica of the 550 Spyder, produced during the late 1980s - very few cars were ever built. Unfortunately, there are no other records available on the company in the author's archives.

TPC

The name given to the Apal during the early stages of its British career, following its launch at the 1984 London Show. For a time, the TPC Motor Company traded from Stratford-upon-Avon, and one of the cars was tested alongside a real 356A by *Classic & Sportscar*. Mike McCarthy noted in his summary of the two machines: "Obviously if you want a car that is eye-catching, either will do. If you want something that is probably more reliable, certainly cheaper to maintain, and behaves like most other current cars, the TPC is the one to own. On the other hand if you want an appreciating asset, a car that delights the senses in a way that only a 356 Porsche can, then go for the original - if you can find one, and if you can afford it."

pable of 107mph and 0-60 in 9.5 seconds.

Frank Reisner later moved to Vancouver, Canada, and is known to have built around 300 Porsche 356A replicas there.

Racing Classic

A fine replica of the 718 Spyder based on VW Beetle mechanical components and built in America under licence from GP Specialist Vehicles in the mid-1980s. Alan Jones (the ex-Grand Prix driver) was trying to get production under way in Australia during the same period.

Sheldonhurst

The British Sheldonhurst concern produced a number of glassfibre-bodied 356 and Speedster replicas. These were offered for sale in 1984 but, unfortunately, the company ran into financial trouble three years later, thus ending the production of Porsche clones and several other projects.

Starborne Speedster

An American-built 356 Speedster replica from around 1980. After a very poor sales response in its native country, the project proved to be very shortlived. However, at least one example was exported to the United Kingdom.

Street Beetle 356 Speedster

This British-built vehicle was developed by Chris and Marcia Boyle, well-known for their VW hot rod conversions. The Speedster could be bought in original 356 form or with the option of 911-style bumpers and wider wheelarches. A

PORSCHE 356

APPENDIX
- PRODUCTION TOTALS
& SPECIFICATIONS

356 Production totals
The total number of 356s built -

356 models 7,627
356A models 21,045
356B models 30,963
356C models 16,678*
Grand total 76,313*
(*including ten extra 356C Dutch police cars)

Specifications
Here are brief specifications of all the Porsches up to and including the first 911s, along with production dates when available. The data is in chronological/engine size order, so that competition cars are listed alongside the contemporary road cars.

Model	Engine Type No.	Capacity (Cylinders)	Bore & Stroke	Power @ rpm	Notes
1948					
356/1100 Coupé		1131cc (4)	75 x 64	40bhp @ 4200	(Gmünd)
356/1100 Cabriolet		1131cc (4)	75 x 64	40bhp @ 4200	(Gmünd)
356/1100 Coupé	369	1086cc (4)	73.5 x 64	40bhp @ 4200	(Gmünd)
356/1100 Cabriolet	369	1086cc (4)	73.5 x 64	40bhp @ 4200	(Gmünd)
1949					
356/1100 Coupé	369	1086cc (4)	73.5 x 64	40bhp @ 4200	(Gmünd)
356/1100 Cabriolet	369	1086cc (4)	73.5 x 64	40bhp @ 4200	(Gmünd)
1950					
356/1100 Coupé	369	1086cc (4)	73.5 x 64	40bhp @ 4200	(Gmünd)
356/1100 Cabriolet	369	1086cc (4)	73.5 x 64	40bhp @ 4200	(Gmünd)
356/1100 Coupé	369	1086cc (4)	73.5 x 64	40bhp @ 4200	(From 4/50)
356/1100 Cabriolet	369	1086cc (4)	73.5 x 64	40bhp @ 4200	(From 4/50)
1951					
356/1100 Coupé	369	1086cc (4)	73.5 x 64	40bhp @ 4200	
356/1100 Cabriolet	369	1086cc (4)	73.5 x 64	40bhp @ 4200	
356/1300 Coupé	506	1286cc (4)	80 x 64	44bhp @ 4200	(From 3/51)
356/1300 Cabriolet	506	1286cc (4)	80 x 64	44bhp @ 4200	(From 3/51)
356/1500 Coupé	527	1488cc (4)	80 x 74	60bhp @ 5000	(From 10/51)
356/1500 Cabriolet	527	1488cc (4)	80 x 74	60bhp @ 5000	(From 10/51)

356 SL Coupé .... 369 .... 1086cc (4) .... 73.5 x 64 .... 46bhp @ 4500 .... (Type 514)

1952
356/1100 Coupé .... 369 .... 1086cc (4) .... 73.5 x 64 .... 40bhp @ 4200
356/1100 Cabriolet .... 369 .... 1086cc (4) .... 73.5 x 64 .... 40bhp @ 4200
356/1300 Coupé .... 506 .... 1286cc (4) .... 80 x 64 .... 44bhp @ 4200
356/1300 Cabriolet .... 506 .... 1286cc (4) .... 80 x 64 .... 44bhp @ 4200
356/1500 Coupé .... 527 .... 1488cc (4) .... 80 x 74 .... 60bhp @ 5000 .... (To 9/52)
356/1500 Cabriolet .... 527 .... 1488cc (4) .... 80 x 74 .... 60bhp @ 5000 .... (To 9/52)
356/1500 Coupé .... 546 .... 1488cc (4) .... 80 x 74 .... 55bhp @ 4400 .... (From 9/52)
356/1500 Cabriolet .... 546 .... 1488cc (4) .... 80 x 74 .... 55bhp @ 4400 .... (From 9/52)
356/1500S Coupé .... 528 .... 1488cc (4) .... 80 x 74 .... 70bhp @ 5500 .... (From 10/52)
356/1500S Cabriolet .... 528 .... 1488cc (4) .... 80 x 74 .... 70bhp @ 5500 .... (From 10/52)
America Roadster .... 528 .... 1488cc (4) .... 80 x 74 .... 70bhp @ 5500 .... (From 4/52)

1953
356/1100 Coupé .... 369 .... 1086cc (4) .... 73.5 x 64 .... 40bhp @ 4200
356/1100 Cabriolet .... 369 .... 1086cc (4) .... 73.5 x 64 .... 40bhp @ 4200
356/1300 Coupé .... 506 .... 1286cc (4) .... 80 x 64 .... 44bhp @ 4200
356/1300 Cabriolet .... 506 .... 1286cc (4) .... 80 x 64 .... 44bhp @ 4200
356/1300S Coupé .... 589 .... 1290cc (4) .... 74.5 x 74 .... 60bhp @ 5500 .... (From 11/53)
356/1300S Cabriolet .... 589 .... 1290cc (4) .... 74.5 x 74 .... 60bhp @ 5500 .... (From 11/53)
356/1500 Coupé .... 546 .... 1488cc (4) .... 80 x 74 .... 55bhp @ 4400
356/1500 Cabriolet .... 546 .... 1488cc (4) .... 80 x 74 .... 55bhp @ 4400
356/1500S Coupé .... 528 .... 1488cc (4) .... 80 x 74 .... 70bhp @ 5500
356/1500S Cabriolet .... 528 .... 1488cc (4) .... 80 x 74 .... 70bhp @ 5500
550 Spyder (works) .... 528 .... 1488cc (4) .... 80 x 74 .... 78bhp @ 6000 .... (From 5/53)
550 Spyder (works) .... 547 .... 1498cc (4) .... 85 x 66 .... 112bhp @ 6200 ..... (From 8/53)

1954
356/1100 Coupé .... 369 .... 1086cc (4) .... 73.5 x 64 .... 40bhp @ 4200 .... (To 12/54)
356/1100 Cabriolet .... 369 .... 1086cc (4) .... 73.5 x 64 .... 40bhp @ 4200 .... (To 12/54)
356/1300 Coupé .... 506 .... 1286cc (4) .... 80 x 64 .... 44bhp @ 4200
356/1300 Cabriolet .... 506 .... 1286cc (4) .... 80 x 64 .... 44bhp @ 4200
356/1300 Speedster .... 506 .... 1286cc (4) .... 80 x 64 .... 44bhp @ 4200 .... (From 9/54)
356/1300 Coupé .... 506/2 .... 1290cc (4) .... 74.5 x 74 .... 44bhp @ 4200 .... (From 11/54)
356/1300 Cabriolet .... 506/2 .... 1290cc (4) .... 74.5 x 74 .... 44bhp @ 4200 .... (From 11/54)
356/1300 Speedster .... 506/2 .... 1290cc (4) .... 74.5 x 74 .... 44bhp @ 4200 .... (From 11/54)
356/1300S Coupé .... 589 .... 1290cc (4) .... 74.5 x 74 .... 60bhp @ 5500 .... (To 5/54)
356/1300S Cabriolet .... 589 .... 1290cc (4) .... 74.5 x 74 .... 60bhp @ 5500 .... (To 5/54)
356/1300A Coupé .... 506/1 .... 1290cc (4) .... 74.5 x 74 .... 44bhp @ 4200 .... (6-11/54)
356/1300A Cabriolet .... 506/1 .... 1290cc (4) .... 74.5 x 74 .... 44bhp @ 4200 .... (6-11/54)
356/1300A Speedster .... 506/1 .... 1290cc (4) .... 74.5 x 74 .... 44bhp @ 4200 .... (9-11/54)
356/1300S Coupé .... 589/2 .... 1290cc (4) .... 74.5 x 74 .... 60bhp @ 5500 .... (From 11/54)
356/1300S Cabriolet .... 589/2 .... 1290cc (4) .... 74.5 x 74 .... 60bhp @ 5500 .... (From 11/54)
356/1300S Speedster .... 589/2 .... 1290cc (4) .... 74.5 x 74 .... 60bhp @ 5500 .... (From 11/54)
356/1500 Coupé .... 546 .... 1488cc (4) .... 80 x 74 .... 55bhp @ 4400 .... (To 11/54)
356/1500 Cabriolet .... 546 .... 1488cc (4) .... 80 x 74 .... 55bhp @ 4400 .... (To 11/54)
356/1500 Speedster .... 546 .... 1488cc (4) .... 80 x 74 .... 55bhp @ 4400 .... (9-11/54)
356/1500 Coupé .... 546/2 .... 1488cc (4) .... 80 x 74 .... 55bhp @ 4400 .... (From 11/54)
356/1500 Cabriolet .... 546/2 .... 1488cc (4) .... 80 x 74 .... 55bhp @ 4400 .... (From 11/54)
356/1500 Speedster .... 546/2 .... 1488cc (4) .... 80 x 74 .... 55bhp @ 4400 .... (From 11/54)
356/1500S Coupé .... 528 .... 1488cc (4) .... 80 x 74 .... 70bhp @ 5500 .... (To 11/54)
356/1500S Cabriolet .... 528 .... 1488cc (4) .... 80 x 74 .... 70bhp @ 5500 .... (To 11/54)
356/1500S Speedster .... 528 .... 1488cc (4) .... 80 x 74 .... 70bhp @ 5500 .... (9-11/54)
356/1500S Coupé .... 528/2 .... 1488cc (4) .... 80 x 74 .... 70bhp @ 5500 .... (From 11/54)
356/1500S Cabriolet .... 528/2 .... 1488cc (4) .... 80 x 74 .... 70bhp @ 5500 .... (From 11/54)
356/1500S Speedster .... 528/2 .... 1488cc (4) .... 80 x 74 .... 70bhp @ 5500 .... (From 11/54)
550 Spyder (customer) .... 528 .... 1488cc (4) .... 80 x 74 .... 100bhp @ 6200

1955

Model	Type	Displacement	Bore x Stroke	Power	Notes
356/1300 Coupé	506/2	1290cc (4)	74.5 x 74	44bhp @ 4200	(To 10/55)
356/1300 Cabriolet	506/2	1290cc (4)	74.5 x 74	44bhp @ 4200	(To 10/55)
356/1300 Speedster	506/2	1290cc (4)	74.5 x 74	44bhp @ 4200	(To 10/55)
356/1300S Coupé	589/2	1290cc (4)	74.5 x 74	60bhp @ 5500	(To 10/55)
356/1300S Cabriolet	589/2	1290cc (4)	74.5 x 74	60bhp @ 5500	(To 10/55)
356/1300S Speedster	589/2	1290cc (4)	74.5 x 74	60bhp @ 5500	(To 10/55)
356/1500 Coupé	546/2	1488cc (4)	80 x 74	55bhp @ 4400	(To 10/55)
356/1500 Cabriolet	546/2	1488cc (4)	80 x 74	55bhp @ 4400	(To 10/55)
356/1500 Speedster	546/2	1488cc (4)	80 x 74	55bhp @ 4400	(To 10/55)
356/1500S Coupé	528/2	1488cc (4)	80 x 74	70bhp @ 5500	(To 10/55)
356/1500S Cabriolet	528/2	1488cc (4)	80 x 74	70bhp @ 5500	(To 10/55)
356/1500S Speedster	528/2	1488cc (4)	80 x 74	70bhp @ 5500	(To 10/55)
356A/1300 Coupé	506/2	1290cc (4)	74.5 x 74	44bhp @ 4200	(From 10/55)
356A/1300 Cabriolet	506/2	1290cc (4)	74.5 x 74	44bhp @ 4200	(From 10/55)
356A/1300 Speedster	506/2	1290cc (4)	74.5 x 74	44bhp @ 4200	(From 10/55)
356A/1300S Coupé	589/2	1290cc (4)	74.5 x 74	60bhp @ 5500	(From 10/55)
356A/1300S Cabriolet	589/2	1290cc (4)	74.5 x 74	60bhp @ 5500	(From 10/55)
356A/1300S Speedster	589/2	1290cc (4)	74.5 x 74	60bhp @ 5500	(From 10/55)
356A/1600 Coupé	616/1	1582cc (4)	82.5 x 74	60bhp @ 4500	(From 10/55)
356A/1600 Cabriolet	616/1	1582cc (4)	82.5 x 74	60bhp @ 4500	(From 10/55)
356A/1600 Speedster	616/1	1582cc (4)	82.5 x 74	60bhp @ 4500	(From 10/55)
356A/1600S Coupé	616/2	1582cc (4)	82.5 x 74	75bhp @ 5000	(From 10/55)
356A/1600S Cabriolet	616/2	1582cc (4)	82.5 x 74	75bhp @ 5000	(From 10/55)
356A/1600S Speedster	616/2	1582cc (4)	82.5 x 74	75bhp @ 5000	(From 10/55)
356A Carrera 1500GS Coupé	547/1	1498cc (4)	85 x 66	100bhp @ 6200	(From 11/55)
356A Carrera 1500GS Cabrio.	547/1	1498cc (4)	85 x 66	100bhp @ 6200	(From 11/55)
356A Carrera 1500GS S/ster	547/1	1498cc (4)	85 x 66	100bhp @ 6200	(From 11/55)
550 Spyder (customer)	528	1488cc (4)	80 x 74	100bhp @ 6200	

1956

Model	Type	Displacement	Bore x Stroke	Power	Notes
356A/1300 Coupé	506/2	1290cc (4)	74.5 x 74	44bhp @ 4200	
356A/1300 Cabriolet	506/2	1290cc (4)	74.5 x 74	44bhp @ 4200	
356A/1300 Speedster	506/2	1290cc (4)	74.5 x 74	44bhp @ 4200	
356A/1300S Coupé	589/2	1290cc (4)	74.5 x 74	60bhp @ 5500	
356A/1300S Cabriolet	589/2	1290cc (4)	74.5 x 74	60bhp @ 5500	
356A/1300S Speedster	589/2	1290cc (4)	74.5 x 74	60bhp @ 5500	
356A/1600 Coupé	616/1	1582cc (4)	82.5 x 74	60bhp @ 4500	
356A/1600 Cabriolet	616/1	1582cc (4)	82.5 x 74	60bhp @ 4500	
356A/1600 Speedster	616/1	1582cc (4)	82.5 x 74	60bhp @ 4500	
356A/1600S Coupé	616/2	1582cc (4)	82.5 x 74	75bhp @ 5000	
356A/1600S Cabriolet	616/2	1582cc (4)	82.5 x 74	75bhp @ 5000	
356A/1600S Speedster	616/2	1582cc (4)	82.5 x 74	75bhp @ 5000	
356A Carrera 1500GS Coupé	547/1	1498cc (4)	85 x 66	100bhp @ 6200	
356A Carrera 1500GS Cabrio.	547/1	1498cc (4)	85 x 66	100bhp @ 6200	
356A Carrera 1500GS S/ster	547/1	1498cc (4)	85 x 66	100bhp @ 6200	
550 Spyder (customer)	528	1488cc (4)	80 x 74	100bhp @ 6200	
550A Spyder	547/2	1498cc (4)	85 x 66	135bhp @ 7200	(From 4/56)

1957

Model	Type	Displacement	Bore x Stroke	Power	Notes
356A/1300 Coupé	506/2	1290cc (4)	74.5 x 74	44bhp @ 4200	(To 9/57)
356A/1300 Cabriolet	506/2	1290cc (4)	74.5 x 74	44bhp @ 4200	(To 9/57)
356A/1300 Speedster	506/2	1290cc (4)	74.5 x 74	44bhp @ 4200	(To 9/57)
356A/1300S Coupé	589/2	1290cc (4)	74.5 x 74	60bhp @ 5500	(To 9/57)
356A/1300S Cabriolet	589/2	1290cc (4)	74.5 x 74	60bhp @ 5500	(To 9/57)
356A/1300S Speedster	589/2	1290cc (4)	74.5 x 74	60bhp @ 5500	(To 9/57)
356A/1600 Coupé	616/1	1582cc (4)	82.5 x 74	60bhp @ 4500	(To 8/57)
356A/1600 Cabriolet	616/1	1582cc (4)	82.5 x 74	60bhp @ 4500	(To 8/57)
356A/1600 Speedster	616/1	1582cc (4)	82.5 x 74	60bhp @ 4500	(To 8/57)
356A/1600S Coupé	616/2	1582cc (4)	82.5 x 74	75bhp @ 5000	(To 8/57)

Model	Type	Capacity	Bore x Stroke	Power	Notes
356A/1600S Cabriolet	616/2	1582cc (4)	82.5 x 74	75bhp @ 5000	(To 8/57)
356A/1600S Speedster	616/2	1582cc (4)	82.5 x 74	75bhp @ 5000	(To 8/57)
356A Carrera 1500GS Coupé	547/1	1498cc (4)	85 x 66	100bhp @ 6200	
356A Carrera 1500GS Cabrio.	547/1	1498cc (4)	85 x 66	100bhp @ 6200	
356A Carrera 1500GS S/ster	547/1	1498cc (4)	85 x 66	100bhp @ 6200	
356A Carrera 1500GT Coupé	547/1	1498cc (4)	85 x 66	110bhp @ 6400	(From 9/57)
356A Carrera 1500GT S/ster	547/1	1498cc (4)	85 x 66	110bhp @ 6400	(From 9/57)
356A/1600 Coupé	616/1	1582cc (4)	82.5 x 74	60bhp @ 4500	(From 9/57)
356A/1600 Cabriolet	616/1	1582cc (4)	82.5 x 74	60bhp @ 4500	(From 9/57)
356A/1600 Speedster	616/1	1582cc (4)	82.5 x 74	60bhp @ 4500	(From 9/57)
356A/1600S Coupé	616/2	1582cc (4)	82.5 x 74	75bhp @ 5000	(From 9/57)
356A/1600S Cabriolet	616/2	1582cc (4)	82.5 x 74	75bhp @ 5000	(From 9/57)
356A/1600S Speedster	616/2	1582cc (4)	82.5 x 74	75bhp @ 5000	(From 9/57)
550A Spyder	547/3	1498cc (4)	85 x 66	142bhp @ 7500	
718 RSK Spyder	547/3	1498cc (4)	85 x 66	142bhp @ 7500	(From 5/57)

1958

Model	Type	Capacity	Bore x Stroke	Power	Notes
356A/1600 Coupé	616/1	1582cc (4)	82.5 x 74	60bhp @ 4500	
356A/1600 Cabriolet	616/1	1582cc (4)	82.5 x 74	60bhp @ 4500	
356A/1600 Speedster	616/1	1582cc (4)	82.5 x 74	60bhp @ 4500	(To 8/58)
356A/1600 Convertible D	616/1	1582cc (4)	82.5 x 74	60bhp @ 4500	(From 8/58)
356A/1600S Coupé	616/2	1582cc (4)	82.5 x 74	75bhp @ 5000	
356A/1600S Cabriolet	616/2	1582cc (4)	82.5 x 74	75bhp @ 5000	
356A/1600S Speedster	616/2	1582cc (4)	82.5 x 74	75bhp @ 5000	(To 8/58)
356A/1600S Convertible D	616/2	1582cc (4)	82.5 x 74	75bhp @ 5000	(From 8/58)
356A Carrera 1500GS Coupé	547/1	1498cc (4)	85 x 66	100bhp @ 6200	(To 8/58)
356A Carrera 1500GS Cabrio.	547/1	1498cc (4)	85 x 66	100bhp @ 6200	(To 8/58)
356A Carrera 1500GS S/ster	547/1	1498cc (4)	85 x 66	100bhp @ 6200	(To 8/58)
356A Carrera 1500GT Coupé	547/1	1498cc (4)	85 x 66	110bhp @ 6400	(To 8/58)
356A Carrera 1500GT S/ster	547/1	1498cc (4)	85 x 66	110bhp @ 6400	(To 8/58)
356A Carrera 1600GS Coupé	692	1587cc (4)	87.5 x 66	105bhp @ 6500	
356A Carrera 1600GS Cabrio.	692	1587cc (4)	87.5 x 66	105bhp @ 6500	
356A Carrera 1600GS S/ster	692	1587cc (4)	87.5 x 66	105bhp @ 6500	(To 8/58)
356A Carrera 1600GT Coupé	692	1587cc (4)	87.5 x 66	115bhp @ 6500	
356A Carrera 1600GT S/ster	692	1587cc (4)	87.5 x 66	115bhp @ 6500	(To 8/58)
718 RSK Spyder	547/3	1498cc (4)	85 x 66	142bhp @ 7500	
718 RSK Spyder	547/4	1587cc (4)	87.5 x 66	160bhp @ 7800	
718 RSK Spyder	547/5	1679cc (4)	90 x 66	170bhp @ 7800	

1959

Model	Type	Capacity	Bore x Stroke	Power	Notes
356A/1600 Coupé	616/1	1582cc (4)	82.5 x 74	60bhp @ 4500	(To 9/59)
356A/1600 Cabriolet	616/1	1582cc (4)	82.5 x 74	60bhp @ 4500	(To 9/59)
356A/1600 Convertible D	616/1	1582cc (4)	82.5 x 74	60bhp @ 4500	(To 9/59)
356A/1600S Coupé	616/2	1582cc (4)	82.5 x 74	75bhp @ 5000	(To 9/59)
356A/1600S Cabriolet	616/2	1582cc (4)	82.5 x 74	75bhp @ 5000	(To 9/59)
356A/1600S Convertible D	616/2	1582cc (4)	82.5 x 74	75bhp @ 5000	(To 9/59)
356A Carrera 1600GS Coupé	692	1587cc (4)	87.5 x 66	105bhp @ 6500	(To 9/59)
356A Carrera 1600GS Cabrio.	692	1587cc (4)	87.5 x 66	105bhp @ 6500	(To 9/59)
356A Carrera 1600GT Coupé	692	1587cc (4)	87.5 x 66	115bhp @ 6500	(To 9/59)
356A Carrera 1600GT S/ster	692	1587cc (4)	87.5 x 66	115bhp @ 6500	(2-9/59)
356B/1600 Coupé	616/1	1582cc (4)	82.5 x 74	60bhp @ 4500	(From 9/59)
356B/1600 Cabriolet	616/1	1582cc (4)	82.5 x 74	60bhp @ 4500	(From 9/59)
356B/1600 Roadster	616/1	1582cc (4)	82.5 x 74	60bhp @ 4500	(From 9/59)
356B/1600S-75 Coupé	616/2	1582cc (4)	82.5 x 74	75bhp @ 5000	(From 9/59)
356B/1600S-75 Cabriolet	616/2	1582cc (4)	82.5 x 74	75bhp @ 5000	(From 9/59)
356B/1600S-75 Roadster	616/2	1582cc (4)	82.5 x 74	75bhp @ 5000	(From 9/59)
718 RSK Spyder	547/3	1498cc (4)	85 x 66	150bhp @ 7800	
718 RSK Spyder	547/4	1587cc (4)	87.5 x 66	160bhp @ 7800	
718 RSK Spyder	547/5	1679cc (4)	90 x 66	170bhp @ 7800	

1960

Model	Type	Displacement	Bore × Stroke	Power	Notes
356B/1600 Coupé	616/1	1582cc (4)	82.5 x 74	60bhp @ 4500	
356B/1600 Cabriolet	616/1	1582cc (4)	82.5 x 74	60bhp @ 4500	
356B/1600 Karmann h/top	616/1	1582cc (4)	82.5 x 74	60bhp @ 4500	(From 8/60)
356B/1600 Roadster	616/1	1582cc (4)	82.5 x 74	60bhp @ 4500	
356B/1600S-75 Coupé	616/2	1582cc (4)	82.5 x 74	75bhp @ 5000	
356B/1600S-75 Cabriolet	616/2	1582cc (4)	82.5 x 74	75bhp @ 5000	
356B/1600S-75 Karmann h/top	616/2	1582cc (4)	82.5 x 74	75bhp @ 5000	(From 8/60)
356B/1600S-75 Roadster	616/2	1582cc (4)	82.5 x 74	75bhp @ 5000	
356B/1600S-90 Coupé	616/7	1582cc (4)	82.5 x 74	90bhp @ 5500	(From 3/60)
356B/1600S-90 Cabriolet	616/7	1582cc (4)	82.5 x 74	90bhp @ 5500	(From 3/60)
356B/1600S-90 Karmann h/top	616/7	1582cc (4)	82.5 x 74	90bhp @ 5500	(From 8/60)
356B/1600S-90 Roadster	616/7	1582cc (4)	82.5 x 74	90bhp @ 5500	(From 3/60)
356B Carrera 1600GT Coupé	692/3A	1587cc (4)	87.5 x 66	134bhp @ 7300	(40 only)
Abarth-Carrera (GTL)	692/3A	1587cc (4)	87.5 x 66	134bhp @ 7300	(20 only)
RS60 Spyder	547/3	1498cc (4)	85 x 66	150bhp @ 7800	
RS60 Spyder	547/4	1587cc (4)	87.5 x 66	160bhp @ 7800	
RS60 Spyder	547/5	1679cc (4)	90 x 66	180bhp @ 7800	
718/2 Formula Two	547/3	1498cc (4)	85 x 66	165bhp @ 8500	

1961

Model	Type	Displacement	Bore × Stroke	Power	Notes
356B/1600 Coupé	616/1	1582cc (4)	82.5 x 74	60bhp @ 4500	(To 9/61)
356B/1600 Cabriolet	616/1	1582cc (4)	82.5 x 74	60bhp @ 4500	(To 9/61)
356B/1600 Karmann h/top	616/1	1582cc (4)	82.5 x 74	60bhp @ 4500	(To 9/61)
356B/1600 Roadster	616/1	1582cc (4)	82.5 x 74	60bhp @ 4500	(To 9/61)
356B/1600S-75 Coupé	616/2	1582cc (4)	82.5 x 74	75bhp @ 5000	(To 9/61)
356B/1600S-75 Cabriolet	616/2	1582cc (4)	82.5 x 74	75bhp @ 5000	(To 9/61)
356B/1600S-75 Karmann h/top	616/2	1582cc (4)	82.5 x 74	75bhp @ 5000	(To 9/61)
356B/1600S-75 Roadster	616/2	1582cc (4)	82.5 x 74	75bhp @ 5000	(To 9/61)
356B/1600S-90 Coupé	616/7	1582cc (4)	82.5 x 74	90bhp @ 5500	(To 9/61)
356B/1600S-90 Cabriolet	616/7	1582cc (4)	82.5 x 74	90bhp @ 5500	(To 9/61)
356B/1600S-90 Karmann h/top	616/7	1582cc (4)	82.5 x 74	90bhp @ 5500	(To 9/61)
356B/1600S-90 Roadster	616/7	1582cc (4)	82.5 x 74	90bhp @ 5500	(To 9/61)
356B/1600 Coupé	616/1	1582cc (4)	82.5 x 74	60bhp @ 4500	(From 9/61)
356B/1600 Cabriolet	616/1	1582cc (4)	82.5 x 74	60bhp @ 4500	(From 9/61)
356B/1600 Karmann h/top	616/1	1582cc (4)	82.5 x 74	60bhp @ 4500	(From 9/61)
356B/1600 Roadster	616/1	1582cc (4)	82.5 x 74	60bhp @ 4500	(From 9/61)
356B/1600S-75 Coupé	616/12	1582cc (4)	82.5 x 74	75bhp @ 5000	(From 9/61)
356B/1600S-75 Cabriolet	616/12	1582cc (4)	82.5 x 74	75bhp @ 5000	(From 9/61)
356B/1600S-75 Karmann h/top	616/12	1582cc (4)	82.5 x 74	75bhp @ 5000	(From 9/61)
356B/1600S-75 Roadster	616/12	1582cc (4)	82.5 x 74	75bhp @ 5000	(From 9/61)
356B/1600S-90 Coupé	616/7	1582cc (4)	82.5 x 74	90bhp @ 5500	(From 9/61)
356B/1600S-90 Cabriolet	616/7	1582cc (4)	82.5 x 74	90bhp @ 5500	(From 9/61)
356B/1600S-90 Karmann h/top	616/7	1582cc (4)	82.5 x 74	90bhp @ 5500	(From 9/61)
356B/1600S-90 Roadster	616/7	1582cc (4)	82.5 x 74	90bhp @ 5500	(From 9/61)
RS61 Spyder	547/3	1498cc (4)	85 x 66	150bhp @ 7800	
RS61 Spyder	547/4	1587cc (4)	87.5 x 66	160bhp @ 7800	
RS61 Spyder	547/5	1679cc (4)	90 x 66	180bhp @ 7800	
RS61 Spyder	547/5	1708cc (4)	90.8 x 66	180bhp @ 7800	
787 Formula One	547/3	1498cc (4)	85 x 66	170bhp @ 9000	

1962

Model	Type	Displacement	Bore × Stroke	Power	Notes
356B/1600 Coupé	616/1	1582cc (4)	82.5 x 74	60bhp @ 4500	
356B/1600 Cabriolet	616/1	1582cc (4)	82.5 x 74	60bhp @ 4500	
356B/1600 Karmann h/top	616/1	1582cc (4)	82.5 x 74	60bhp @ 4500	(To 6/62)
356B/1600 Roadster	616/1	1582cc (4)	82.5 x 74	60bhp @ 4500	(To 6/62)
356B/1600S-75 Coupé	616/12	1582cc (4)	82.5 x 74	75bhp @ 5000	
356B/1600S-75 Cabriolet	616/12	1582cc (4)	82.5 x 74	75bhp @ 5000	
356B/1600S-75 Karmann h/top	616/12	1582cc (4)	82.5 x 74	75bhp @ 5000	(To 6/62)
356B/1600S-75 Roadster	616/12	1582cc (4)	82.5 x 74	75bhp @ 5000	(To 6/62)

356B/1600S-90 Coupé .... 616/7 .... 1582cc (4) .... 82.5 x 74 .... 90bhp @ 5500
356B/1600S-90 Cabriolet .... 616/7 .... 1582cc (4) .... 82.5 x 74 .... 90bhp @ 5500
356B/1600S-90 Karmann h/top ...... 616/7 .... 1582cc (4) .... 82.5 x 74 .... 90bhp @ 5500 .... (To 6/62)
356B/1600S-90 Roadster .... 616/7 .... 1582cc (4) .... 82.5 x 74 .... 90bhp @ 5500 .... (To 6/62)
Carrera 2/2000GS Coupé .... 587/1 .... 1966cc (4) .... 92 x 74 .... 130bhp @ 6200 ..... (From 4/62)
804 Formula One .... 753 .... 1494cc (8) .... 66 x 54.6 .... 185bhp @ 9200

1963
356B/1600 Coupé .... 616/1 .... 1582cc (4) .... 82.5 x 74 .... 60bhp @ 4500 .... (To 7/63)
356B/1600 Cabriolet .... 616/1 .... 1582cc (4) .... 82.5 x 74 .... 60bhp @ 4500 .... (To 7/63)
356B/1600S-75 Coupé .... 616/12 .... 1582cc (4) .... 82.5 x 74 .... 75bhp @ 5000 .... (To 7/63)
356B/1600S-75 Cabriolet .... 616/12 .... 1582cc (4) .... 82.5 x 74 .... 75bhp @ 5000 .... (To 7/63)
356B/1600S-90 Coupé .... 616/7 .... 1582cc (4) .... 82.5 x 74 .... 90bhp @ 5500 .... (To 7/63)
356B/1600S-90 Cabriolet .... 616/7 .... 1582cc (4) .... 82.5 x 74 .... 90bhp @ 5500 .... (To 7/63)
Carrera 2/2000GS Coupé .... 587/1 .... 1966cc (4) .... 92 x 74 .... 130bhp @ 6200 ..... (To 7/63)
2000 GS/GT .... 587/1 .... 1966cc (4) .... 92 x 74 .... 155bhp @ 7800
356C/1600C Coupé .... 616/15 .... 1582cc (4) .... 82.5 x 74 .... 75bhp @ 5200 .... (From 7/63)
356C/1600C Cabriolet..................... 616/15 .... 1582cc (4) .... 82.5 x 74 .... 75bhp @ 5200 .... (From 7/63)
356C/1600SC Coupé .... 616/16 .... 1582cc (4) .... 82.5 x 74 .... 95bhp @ 5800 .... (From 7/63)
356C/1600SC Cabriolet .... 616/16 .... 1582cc (4) .... 82.5 x 74 .... 95bhp @ 5800 .... (From 7/63)
Carrera 2/2000GS Coupé .... 587/1 .... 1966cc (4) .... 92 x 74 .... 130bhp @ 6200 ..... (From 7/63)
904GTS.. 587/3 .... 1966cc (4) .... 92 x 74 .... 180bhp @ 7000
904GTS/6 .... 901 .... 1991cc (6) .... 80 x 66 .... 210bhp @ 8000
904GTS/8 .... 771 .... 1981cc (8) .... 76 x 54.6 .... 230bhp @ 9000

1964
356C/1600C Coupé .... 616/15 .... 1582cc (4) .... 82.5 x 74 .... 75bhp @ 5200
356C/1600C Cabriolet..................... 616/15 .... 1582cc (4) .... 82.5 x 74 .... 75bhp @ 5200
356C/1600SC Coupé .... 616/16 .... 1582cc (4) .... 82.5 x 74 .... 95bhp @ 5800
356C/1600SC Cabriolet .... 616/16 .... 1582cc (4) .... 82.5 x 74 .... 95bhp @ 5800
Carrera 2/2000GS Coupé .... 587/1 .... 1966cc (4) .... 92 x 74 .... 130bhp @ 6200
911 De Luxe .... 901/01 .... 1991cc (6) .... 80 x 66 .... 130bhp @ 6100 ..... (From 9/64)

1965
356C/1600C Coupé .... 616/15 .... 1582cc (4) .... 82.5 x 74 .... 75bhp @ 5200 .... (To 4/65)
356C/1600C Cabriolet..................... 616/15 .... 1582cc (4) .... 82.5 x 74 .... 75bhp @ 5200 .... (To 4/65)
356C/1600SC Coupé .... 616/16 .... 1582cc (4) .... 82.5 x 74 .... 95bhp @ 5800 .... (To 4/65)
356C/1600SC Cabriolet .... 616/16 .... 1582cc (4) .... 82.5 x 74 .... 95bhp @ 5800 .... (To 4/65)
Carrera 2/2000GS Coupé .... 587/1 .... 1966cc (4) .... 92 x 74 .... 130bhp @ 6200 ..... (To 4/65)
911 De Luxe .... 901/01 .... 1991cc (6) .... 80 x 66 .... 130bhp @ 6100
912 .... 616/16 .... 1582cc (4) .... 82.5 x 74 .... 90bhp @ 5800 .... (From 5/65)
Spyder .... 771 .... 1981cc (8) .... 76 x 54.6 .... 240bhp @ 9000

1966
356C/1600SC Cabriolet .... 616/16 .... 1582cc (4) .... 82.5 x 74 .... 95bhp @ 5800 .... (Ten only)
911 De Luxe .... 901/01 .... 1991cc (6) .... 80 x 66 .... 130bhp @ 6100 ..... (To 9/66)
912 .... 616/16 .... 1582cc (4) .... 82.5 x 74 .... 90bhp @ 5800
906 (Carrera 6) .... 901 .... 1991cc (6) .... 80 x 66 .... 210bhp @ 8000 ..... (From 1/66)
906 2.2 .... 771 .... 2195cc (8) .... 80 x 54.6 .... 260bhp @ 8600
910 Berg .... 771 .... 1981cc (8) .... 76 x 54.6 .... 272bhp @ 9000

PORSCHE 356

INDEX

The Porsche company and its products are mentioned throughout the book.